For those who enjoyed ~~Rugby Jokes~~, ~~More~~
Rugby Jokes and *What Rugby Jokes Did Next*,
Sphere present even *More Rugby Jokes*.
And don't forget to watch out for *Rugby Songs*
and *More Rugby Songs*.

More Rugby Jokes

SPHERE BOOKS LIMITED
30–32 Gray's Inn Road, London WC1X 8JL

First published in Great Britain by
Sphere Books Ltd 1984
Copyright © E.L.Ranelagh 1984

TRADE
MARK

Set in Baskerville

Printed and bound in Great Britain by
Cox & Wyman Ltd, Reading

Contents

Scoring, or Trying To

ON THE TRAIN

A guard on a railway train was telling how you can never trust a woman.

Seems once he noticed that there was a girl all alone in a compartment. Then at a later station, he noticed that a man got on the train, sat in the same compartment, and started reading his newspaper. A little later the two of them were talking. When the guard looked again, they had pulled down the blinds.

Presently, her scarf was thrown out of the window. Then, after fairly long intervals, came her pull-over and then her blouse. After that, it was her skirt that went out. And then it was her slip. Next her bra. Next one stocking and then the other. Then her garter-belt. Then her panties.

'And *then*,' he said, 'she pulled the alarm cord!'

RAPE

A man came out of a supermarket staggering under a big sack of potatoes, another big sack of onions, a twenty-pound ham, and two awkward paper bags spilling over with groceries. A pretty girl was walking ahead of him as he made his way toward his car.

'Excuse me, miss,' he said. 'Could you stop for a moment and open the boot of my car for me?'

'No,' she said. 'I could not.'

'Why?'

'Because you might rape me.'

The man was flabbergasted. 'Rape you! How could I possibly rape you, loaded down as I am?'

'Well,' she said, 'you could always put down the two sacks and then put the bags on top, and I could hold the ham.'

ABTHOLUTELY DIVINE

The god Thor had a habit of looking over the country for pretty women. He would choose the prettiest. Then at night he would appear in her bed and have his way with her. He never revealed that he was really a god.

Once he found a very beautiful girl, and all during that night he had a marvellous time, the best time ever. It was so good that in the morning he felt he must reward her.

He decided that the best way to show his great favour would be to tell her who he was.

So after an impressive silence, he said, 'I'm Thor, darling!'

'Tho am I,' said she, 'but I'm thatithfied.'

SLOW WORK

A Russian's idea of a date was to strip the girl, strip himself, and have at it.

An English friend took him aside and told him that in this country, this would not do. There should first be some conversation about art or nature or such things; and that only after that should he put the proposition.

So the Russian drove out with a girl.

'Nize country,' he said. She nodded.

A few miles later, 'Nize trees.' She nodded again.

A few miles further on, 'Nize sheep.' She nodded.

He stopped the car. 'Enough of zis loff-making. Strip!'

MUSTN'T BE OVERHEARD

There was a dance at a school for the deaf and dumb. A visitor thought the dancing very well done, but he was especially interested in the gesticulations of the dancers. He kept asking an interpreter to translate what their fingers were saying.

Later on he noticed two young men in a corner. One had his hand half hidden under his tie and was moving his fingers wildly.

'What's he doing?'

'Oh him! He's telling dirty stories.'

LEGAL

Three girls thought they'd have some fun, so they put a sign on the back of their car, THREE YOUNG MEN WANTED.

But a policeman noticed the sign and stopped them. 'It's illegal to have a sign like that on your car,' he said.

'What's wrong with it?'

'It's immoral,' he said.

Just then a car drove past with a big sign on the back saying JESUS SAVES.

'See that?' said the girls. 'How come that one is legal and ours isn't?'

'That sign is moral,' said the policeman.

The girls said no more.

But the next day the policeman noticed the same three girls. This time though, there was a different sign on the rear of their car, a big one. It read THREE LITTLE ANGELS LOOKING FOR SAINT PETER.

GREETING

Girl to date: 'Hello, tall, dark and hands.'

YOU HAVE BEEN WARNED

A department store was adding an extension. In the course of the work large signs were hung on the walls and in some cases over the backs of seats, advising the public about the changes.

A pretty young woman sat down on one of these chairs, and somehow the cord from the sign on it got looped over a button on the back of her collar. As she stood up and then as she walked smartly down the street, those behind her could read, BECAUSE OF ALTERATIONS TO THE FRONT, ENTRANCE IS NOW FROM THE REAR.

NEW WAY

It is very late on a moonlit winter night. A pair o
anxious parents, bundled up against the cold, are
standing at the foot of a ladder which is leaning against
an open window on the first floor.

The father is saying to the mother, 'Are you sure
they're eloping? He's been up there four hours!'

LITERARY TYPES (1)

ODE TO A FOUR-LETTER EXPLETIVE DELETED

Though a lady repel your advance, she'll be kind
As long as you intimate what's on your mind.
You can tell her you're hungry and need to be swung,
You can ask her to see how your etchings are hung.
You may mention the ashes that need to be hauled,
Put the lid on her saucepan, even lay's not too bald.
But the minute you're forthright, get ready to duck –
*The girl isn't born yet who'll stand for 'Let's ****.'*

LITERARY TYPES (2)

SHORT SHORT STORY

The Salesman: Listen, I'm only in town for a few hours and I can't kid around. Do you screw or don't you?

The Girl (shyly): Well, I don't normally, but you've talked me into it.

LITERARY TYPES (3)

ADVERT FOR A SUMMER RESORT

'This is a Honeymoon Heaven! Try a weekend first.'

LITERARY TYPES (4)

LOVE POEM

Slim's girl is tall and slender,
  My girl is short and low.
Slim's girl wears silks and satins,
  My girl wears calico.
Slim's girl is rich and sporty,
  My girl is poor and good.
Would I trade girls with Slim?
  You're God-damned right I would!

APARTMENT FOR RENT

A prosperous business man propositioned a beautifu chorus girl. She agreed to spend the night with him for £500.

When he was ready to leave, he told her that he didn't have the money with him, but he would have his secretary write a cheque for it and mail it to her calling it 'Rent for Apartment.'

On the way to the office the following morning, he decided the whole thing wasn't worth the price he had agreed to pay. So he had his secretary send a cheque for £250 and the following note:

Dear Madam,

Enclosed please find cheque in the amount of £250 for the rent of your flat. I am not sending the amount agreed upon because when I rented the flat I was under the impression that

1.   It had never been occupied.
2.   That there was plenty of heat.
3.   That it was small.

Last night I found that it had been previously occupied, that there wasn't any heat at all, and that it was entirely too large.

Yours truly.

On the receipt of the note, the girl immediately returned the cheque with the following:

Dear Sir,

I cannot understand how you can expect a beautiful flat to remain unoccupied. As for the heat, there is plenty, if you know how to turn it on. As for the size, it is not my fault that you didn't have enough furniture to furnish it.

Yours truly.

A man looks around in a bar, sees an attractive girl and offers her a drink.

'Did you say a motel?' she asks him in a very loud voice.

He nervously tries to explain that what he had suggested was a drink.

She shrieks, 'You want to take me to a motel?'

The clientele in the bar stare at him. The barman says, 'Steady there!' He is mortified and slinks away to a table in the corner where he sits by himself.

Later on, the girl comes over to him. 'I must apologise. I hope I didn't embarrass you too much. You see, I'm a Psychology student, and I wanted to take notes on your reaction for my term paper.'

The man shouts, 'Twenty pounds? You must be joking!'

RELATIVITY

Said Einstein, 'I have an equation
Which science might call Rabelaisian:
Let P be virginity
Approaching infinity,
And U be a constant persuasion.
Now if P over V be inverted,
And the square root of U be inserted
X times over P,
The result Q E D,
Is a relative,' Einstein asserted.

NEW PROVERBS FOR OLD

Early to bed and early to rise,
And your girl will go out with additional guys.

GROUCHO

Groucho Marx was boasting about his statistics. The other fellow then detailed all his own achievements and finally asked, 'Now, can you beat that?'

'Easy,' said Groucho. 'I'll do it with one example only: I got out of bed one morning, and wearing only my pyjama-trousers went down two flights of stairs to the front door, picked up a bottle of milk in each hand, and went back up the stairs again.'

'What's so remarkable about that?'

'There was no belt on my pyjamas.'

Y SCOUTS

The Boy Scouts had made camp after a long hike, and that evening they sat round the campfire for some rest and recreation. Two of them began comparing notes.

Scout A: Mine's bigger than yours.
Scout B: Mine's a lot longer than yours!
Scout A: No, mine's a lot longer than yours.
Scout B: No, your sister told my sister that mine's a lot bigger than yours.
Scout A: OK then, let's measure them.

They took off their belts and hung them side by side.

CHOOSY

Jim and Andy made a pastime of looking over the girls wherever and whenever they saw them, and then dismissing them with various degrees of non-interest.

Once Jim seemed to take special notice. 'See that one?' he asked.

Andy was surprised, so he looked her over well. 'What about her?'

'I wouldn't even use yours on her!'

RIGHT!

A fat man was seated on a bus. Two women were sitting opposite him. One of them, eyeing him, whispered to her friend, 'Now if that stomach was on a woman, it would indicate pregnancy!'

The man overheard her. Smiling, he said, 'Lady, it was, and she is.'

A TOAST

Here's to the men.
When I meet 'em, I like 'em,
When I like 'em, I kiss 'em,
When I kiss 'em, I love 'em,
When I love 'em, I let 'em,
When I let 'em, I lose 'em.
    God-damn 'em!

Caviar comes from virgin sturgeon,
Virgin sturgeon's a very fine dish.
Virgin sturgeon needs no urgin'
That's why caviar's my favourite dish.

I fed caviar to my girl friend,
She was a virgin tried and true.
Now my girl friend needs no urgin'
There isn't anything she won't do.

I fed caviar to my grandpa,
He was a gent of ninety-three.
Shrieks and squeals revealed that grandpa
Had chased grandma up a tree.

Shad roe comes from scarlet shad fish,
Shad fish have a sorry fate.
Pregnant shad fish is a sad fish,
Got that way without a mate.

The green sea-turtle's mate is happy
With her lover's winning ways.
First he grips her with his flippers,
Then he grips and flips for days.

Mrs Clam is optimistic,
Shoots her eggs out in the sea,
Hopes her suitor is a shooter
With the self-same shot as she.

Give a thought to the happy codfish,
Always there when duty calls.
Female codfish is an odd fish,
From them come the codfish balls.

Oysters they are fleshy bivalves,
They have youngsters in their shell.
How they diddle is a riddle,
But they do, so what the hell.

VIOLATE ME

Violate me, in violet time,
In the vilest way that you know.
Ruin me, ravish me,
Brutally, savagely,
To me no mercy show.

To other men I am
Rude and oblivious,
Give me a man who is
Lewd and lascivious.
Violate me, in violet time,
In the vilest way that you know.

Marriage

MODERN TIMES

Boy: Fancy meeting you here!

Girl (glumly): Oh hello.

Boy: Did you enjoy that smashing meeting we went to at the British Butterfly Collectors Convention?

Girl: Er – yes.

Boy: We must do it again sometime.

Girl: I'd love to, but well, I must dash!

Boy: But you're in a bus queue.

Girl: Oh, so I am! I just remembered that I've got to go. See you!

Boy: When?

Girl: Oh some time next month or something.

Boy: Let's set a date.

Girl: Well, phone me.

Boy: But you're not on the phone.

Girl: Well?

Boy: It's just a piece of good luck that we bumped into each other. That's why we should fix a date now.

Girl: Oh, I just can't say.

Boy: How about tomorrow:

Girl: I'm washing my hair.

Boy: After that?

Girl: Drying my hair.

Boy: How about Wednesday?

Girl: No, I can't make it. It's my brother's birthday.

Boy: You haven't got a brother.

Girl: Oh, silly me! It's my cousin's birthday – he's like a brother to me.

Boy: Thursday then?

Girl: I'll be working late at the office.

Boy: Friday?

Girl: I'll be working late at the office.

Boy: Saturday?
Girl: Working late at the office.
Boy: Sunday?
Girl: Working late at the office.
Boy: Always the same excuse.
Girl: I can't think of any other.
Boy: You don't say! You know, sometimes I wonder if you want to go out with me. I can't really think why we got married.

HIS PART

The wife wasn't well, so her husband went with her to the doctor. After the examination, the doctor sent her out and asked the husband to come in.

'Your wife's trouble is that she needs more sex. I'm prescribing sex three times a week.'

'Well, put me down for every other Thursday.'

ADVICE TO BRIDEGROOMS

A groom-to-be was completely ignorant about marriage and very anxious to learn everything he should know.

At last he told his troubles to a neighbour. This man explained as best he could, and then suggested that the young man try it first with a calf.

Some months passed before the two met again. 'Well,' asked the neighbour, 'how did it go? I'm sure you're now happy in your marriage.'

'Oh,' came the reply, 'I didn't get married after all. It's cheaper with a calf.'

WEDDING NIGHT

On the first night, the newly married pair were ready to retire. The husband quickly undressed and got into bed.

But the wife first removed her contact lenses. She put them in the drawer. Then she took off her eyelashes and put them in the drawer. Then she took out her dentures and put those in the drawer. Her wig went in the drawer too. Next she removed her falsies, and she even had on some hip-padding as well. These all went in the drawer.

Then her husband got up.

She said, 'Now where are you going?'

He said, 'I'm going to get in that drawer.'

ANOTHER FIT

A boy happened to see his parents in the bedroom, and as soon as he had a chance, he asked his father about it. 'Dad, when I passed by your room last night, it looked as if you and mother were wrestling.'

'Oh, no son. Your mother was having a fit and I was holding her down.'

'Oh.'

A couple of days later, when the father came home, his son ran down the hall crying, 'Daddy, Daddy, Daddy, Daddy!'

'What's wrong, son?'

'Daddy, mother had another one of those fits today, and the milkman held her down.'

MORMON WEDDING

Pastor to groom: Do you take these women to be your wives?

Groom: I do.

Pastor to brides: Do you take this man to be your husband?

Brides: We do.

Pastor: Some of you girls in the back will have to speak up louder if you want to be included.

SHE WAS RIGHT

A fellow was determined to marry a virgin. His trick was to take a girl out driving, unzip his pants, and ask her what she saw. If she called it by its right name, he had no more to do with her.

One day he met a young pretty girl, drove out with her, and went through the usual routine. When he asked her what was the thing she saw, she giggled and said, 'Oh, it's a tee-hee!'

He was very pleased, proposed then and there, and the wedding took place soon after.

That night in the bedroom he undressed and said, 'Now darling, here is something you should learn. This is a prick.'

'Oh no,' she said, 'it's a tee-hee. Every prick I ever saw was much bigger than that!'

AT THE HOSPITAL

An elderly lord is in the waiting-room of a big London hospital while his wife is giving birth. He is reading a newspaper.

A nurse comes in to say, 'Congratulations, your Lordship! Her Ladyship has just had a baby boy.' He keeps on reading.

A little while later the nurse appears again, all smiles. 'Isn't it splendid, sir! Her Ladyship has had another boy!' He keeps on reading.

It happens a third time. The nurse rushes out. 'Your Lordship, your Lordship! Her Ladyship has just had a third son – triplets!'

He looks up.

He speaks! 'Roomy old bitch.'

A THOUGHT

Incompatibility is not such a bad thing in marriage, especially if he has income and she is pattable.

NOT HER FAULT

A stranger came to town, saw Ed's pretty wife, and told her he'd give her five hundred pounds if he could sleep with her. She dutifully reported all this to Ed, and he decided it would be worth it.

It happened that Ed and his brother had to go away on business, so it was easy for Ed's wife to make the arrangements, and she got the five hundred pounds.

But it was her sister, not so pretty, who was married to Ed's brother, who was the one who got a scolding from her husband.

'How come you can't do what your sister does?'

'It's not my fault,' she protested. 'I do do it! More often than she does, too! And better! The mayor and the chief councilman sleep with me, each of them twice a week! It's just a detail that they don't pay me.'

SIMPLE

One night a Colonel, a Major and a Captain were having an argument about marriage. The Colonel said that marriage was 60% work and 40% fun. The Major disagreed – according to him it was 75% work and 25% fun. The Captain's view was that it might be 90% work and 10% fun.

At this point an orderly happened to appear. 'Let's leave it to him,' said the Colonel.

They called him over. The orderly listened carefully to each of them. Then he said with quiet finality, 'If you will pardon me, sirs, you are all wrong. Marriage is 100% fun and no work at all.'

'How do you figure that?' the three wanted to know.

'It's very simple. If there were any work in it, you fellows would have me doing it.'

REPORT

In a country town in France, the curé was carrying on with the wife of a shopkeeper. She went to church on every occasion, and the curé made pastoral visits whenever he could, but it wasn't enough.

The shopkeeper began to have suspicions. Then one day his wife had a toothache, and she insisted on going to the curé instead of to the doctor. Without making any accusations in front of their young son, the shopkeeper sent the child to watch what went on during this treatment. The boy climbed a tree outside a window of the curé's house.

'What happened?' asked the father when the boy returned.

'Oh, the curé took a long big tooth out of mother's stomach.'

WHAT'S FITTING

In bed, the French bride asks the husband what his balls are for.

'Oh,' he replies, 'they are for show.'

After several goes, she is still restless. 'Chéri,' she says, 'we are, after all, simple bourgeois and little used to show. Put the show in as well!'

ANYTHING'S BETTER THAN WORK

One of the workmen asked the boss if he could get off tomorrow.

'You know we're short-handed. Seems to me you had time off six or seven weeks ago.'

'Yes, that's right. It was to go to my wife's funeral.'

'Well, why do you want to get off tomorrow?'

'So I can get married.'

'Married! That's a bit much. Your wife hasn't been in her grave for two months!'

'Well, I never was one to hold a grudge long.'

VENETIANS

A courtesan in Venice was asked which nationality had the biggest equipment.

She replied, 'The Venetians of course. They are so long that though they are often away in distant lands, they are still able to connect with their wives and produce children. The children are here to prove it!'

FURTHER PROOF

A Florentine who lived in Venice made a similar remark. His Venetian friends were all merchants and consequently away for months at a time. They used to say that his children were skinny and weak compared with theirs.

He said, 'But I work alone at the making of my children, while you have a number of assistants!'

A DEAL

A father is very pleased when his daughter starts going out with a very rich young man. But his day-dreams are shattered when his wife tells him what the daughter has told her – that this young man has made her pregnant.

The father is furious. He goes straight away to see the man and threatens to kill him.

'Calm down, calm down,' says the man. 'Don't get excited. I will do the right thing by your daughter. If it's a boy, I will settle a hundred thousand pounds on him. If it's a girl, I'll give her seventy thousand. Now what do you think of that?'

'And if it's a miscarriage,' asks the father, 'will you give her another chance?'

HOW TO TELL A SELF-MADE TYCOON

1st.   He quits shining his own shoes.
2nd.   He quits writing his own letters.
3rd.   He quits writing his own speeches.
4th.   He quits making love to his own wife.

A DRAW

A continental lady who had married an Englishman and lived in England for a long time happened to meet on the street in London an old childhood friend whom she hadn't seen nor been in touch with for years.

'How are you! How are you!' they cried, and they had a fine time recalling their youth and catching up with each other's news.

'And have you any children?' the old friend asked.

'Of course!' replied the first one. 'Two, a daughter and a son. Both are in England, and now my daughter is married.'

'Is she happily married?'

'Oh, she is very well fixed! Every morning her husband gets up early and turns on the central heating, and then he makes breakfast for her and brings it on a tray to her in bed. And every evening when he comes home from work, he does the washing-up for her! It's lovely.'

'And your son?'

'He is married too. It's such a pity. Every morning he has to get up early and turn on the heat, and then he has to make breakfast for his wife and bring it up to her in bed. And when he comes home from work he has to do the washing-up! It's a shame, that's what it is!'

BROKER

Danny Paddy Andy Donohue was famous as the most successful marriage-broker in the west of Ireland. They say that in his time he arranged over four hundred marriages and was thus instrumental in bringing into the world at least sixteen-hundred children. God rest him!

One day he approached a poor young bachelor. He told him he had a great opportunity for him. There was this girl from a fine family, an only daughter, and five hundred acres went with her! What's more, she was young and beautiful.

'Sure, Danny Paddy Andy, she's too good for me. She'd niver have me.'

'Don't ye worry yerself about that, me lad. She would.'

The young man couldn't figure it out. He thought for a while.

'If she's such good value,' he said, 'what would she want with me? What's the catch?'

'Sure there's a catch,' said Danny Paddy Andy, 'but it's nothing much, nothing much at all, at all.'

'What is it then?'

'It's just that she's the least little bit pregnant.'

THE CHILD WAS NOT ASLEEP

A Russian peasant couple slept with their small son on his mattress right next to their bed. One night the father was especially keen, and he refused to listen to his wife's warnings that the child was not yet asleep.

They were hard at it when there was a great banging at the front door.

The father was about to jump up and open it when the child said, 'Keep f***king, Papa, it's just the pig knocking about.'

MEASURING UP

A couple were in bed when a storm started. The rain was coming in through the window, and neither of them wanted to get up and close it. 'You do it,' said the husband.

'No, you do it.'

'Well,' he said, 'if I can make up a better crack than you, then you close the window.'

She agreed, and so he said:

Three and three make six.
Six and three make nine.
I can get into yours,
But you can't get into mine.

The wife was annoyed. She got up and closed the window, but she couldn't sleep.

'I can do better than that,' she said to herself. Finally she thought of a better one. She jumped up and opened the window. Then she woke up her husband.

'Darling,' she said, 'get up and close the window.'

'What do you mean?' he said. 'We've finished with that bit.'

'No, we haven't. I've got a better crack:

Three and three make six.
Six and three make nine.
I can measure yours,
But you can't measure mine.'

INHERITANCE

Because his son's tutor seduced his daughter, the father quickly marries her to another.

Four months later she has a baby. The new husband protests, but the father consoles him with money.

'The same thing happened to me,' he says. 'Keep the money for *your* daughter.'

MOTHER-IN-LAW (1)

On their wedding-night the young couple went to bed in the bride's home, where all had been laid out for them. The groom put on the fine night-shirt waiting for him on the pillow, but he couldn't fit his head into the nightcap.

He said to the bride, 'I can't get into this.'

The mother-in-law, listening at the door, cried out, 'Marie, open your legs!'

MOTHER-IN-LAW (2)

Another bride was wearing elegant shoes bought to go with her wedding dress, but unfortunately they were very tight. When she started to undress to go to bed, try as she might, she couldn't get the shoes off.

The groom helped her as best he could, but though they pulled and pushed, the shoes remained on. Finally the groom said, 'We'll have to use a knife.'

'No! No!' screamed the mother-in-law from the next room. 'Use butter first!'

MOTHER-IN-LAW (3)

While in the bride's home the wedding-party was still going strong, the mother-in-law was putting the last touches on the matrimonial bedchamber. She found some brandy that the bridegroom had left there and helped herself to a good drink. Then she rejoined the festivities.

Hours later, when the young couple had retired, the groom in due course went to take a drink himself and was startled to find the bottle no longer full.

'Somebody's been hitting this thing!' he said to the bride.

Mother-in-law from the next room: 'No, it's just that we're big there in this family.'

THE SADDLE

A portrait painter is sent for by a rich patron. He has to go to the patron's home in the city for a fairly long stay.

But before he leaves, he amuses himself by painting a mule on his wife's front.

'There! That will warn others to stay off the grass,' he says. He kisses his wife goodbye and departs.

Hardly is he gone when the wife's lover comes to call, and in the weeks that follow, he calls again and again. Eventually it is time for the husband to return, and the couple discover that the mule has been quite worn off.

There is nothing for it except for the lover to paint on a new mule. This he does, but having forgotten the details, he paints a saddle on the mule.

The husband returns, and that night accuses his wife of adultery during his absence.

> 'Can you distrust me?' Chloe cries,
> 'Inhuman man!' and wipes her eyes.
> 'The mule, I see, is safe, my dear,
> But zounds! who put the saddle here?'

HE CALLED THE WEDDING OFF

A boy was fixing to get married, but just a few days before the wedding he said the whole thing was called off.

His father wanted to know what went wrong. 'Well', said the son, 'I found out she is a virgin. That's why I decided not to marry her.'

'Son,' said the old man, 'you done right. If that girl ain't good enough for her own kinfolks, she ain't good enough for us.'

TACT

An Austrian couple wanted to celebrate after their wedding, so they decided to go on a trip. The big town they went to was full of festivity and visitors, and it was only after a long search that they found on the edge of town an inn which had one room left.

The host said the room was comfortable and the view very pleasant. The groom said that provided the service was good, they would take it. As for that, the host assured them that the house servant was very resourceful.

That night when the couple wanted to go to bed, they found that their room was far from all the inn's facilities, and that there was not even a chamber-pot in the room.

The husband rang for the servant. 'We need a chamber-pot.'

The servant said that none was available; all were in use. 'But do not worry. I will look.'

After a short time he returned. Invisible, he opened the door only enough to slip his right hand through. In it he was holding a big vinegar-bottle which he silently set down.

'But what about my wife?'

Still silently, this time he put his left hand through. In it was a funnel.

EVENING WEAR

After dinner the wife put on a strapless, plunging, slit-skirt evening gown to go to a party.

'I'm so tired,' she said to her husband. 'I don't really feel like going.'

'All right, dear,' he said. 'Then put something on and we'll go to bed.'

CAUSE FOR DIVORCE

A newly-married son-in-law says to his father-in-law, 'I want a divorce.'

'Why? You're only just married!'

'I want a divorce because your daughter has no hair where there should be hair.'

'Is that all?' said the girl's father. 'That's nothing.'

'No, it's not nothing! Your wife has plenty, I've been told by my father, my uncles and various others. It's all the same to me, but my friends will make fun of me – one without hair!'

EXPLAINED

Did you hear about the woman who got married four times?

The first was a millionaire.

The second was a famous actor.

The third was a well-known minister.

The fourth was an undertaker.

I get it! One for the money, two for the show, three to get ready, and four to go.

DIARY

A man writes in his diary:

I am an exemplary man. I neither smoke nor drink. I never go to night clubs. I am loyal to my wife and do not flirt. I go to bed at eight o'clock and rise early. I work regular hours and exercise daily.

But all this is going to change as soon as I get out of jail.

BUTTONS ON A BLANKET

When I came home last Saturday night,
As drunk as drunk could be,
I saw a hat upon the rack
Where my hat ought to be.
'Come hither, my wife, come hither,
Explain this thing to me.
How come this hat upon the rack
Where my hat ought to be?'

'You damn fool, you silly fool,
You're drunk as drunk could be.
That's nothing but a chamber-pot
My mother sent to me.'
'Now in all my years of travel,
A million miles or more,
A John B. Stetson chamber-pot
I never saw before.'

When I came home last Saturday night,
As drunk as drunk can be,
I saw some pants laid on the chair
Where my pants ought to be.
'Come hither, my wife, come hither,
Explain this thing to me.
How come these pants upon the chair
Where my pants ought to be?'

'You damn fool, you silly fool,
You're drunk as drunk can be.
That's nothing but a blanket
My mother sent to me.'
'Now in all my years of travel,
A million miles or more,
Buttons on a blanket,
I never saw before.'

When I came home last Saturday night,
As drunk as drunk can be,
I saw a head upon my bed
Where my head ought to be.
'Come hither, my wife, come hither,
Explain this thing to me.
How come this head upon the bed
Where my head ought to be?'

'You damn fool, you silly fool,
You're drunk as drunk could be.
That's nothing but a cabbage,
My mother sent to me.'
'Now in all my years of travel,
A million miles or more,
A moustache on a cabbage
I never saw before.'

You're Never Too Old and You're Never Too Young

RIDDEN, NOT WRITTEN

When a spry old maiden lady in a country village reached the age of one hundred, reporters from the city newspapers came out to interview her.

One of them said to her, 'Is it true, Aunt Nellie, that you've never been bedridden?'

'Of course it isn't, young man!' she said. 'I've been bed-ridden, and I've been carriage-ridden, and I've even been car-ridden, but you needn't put any of that in your story.'

NOW IT'S REALLY BAD

On the front steps of his home, which happened to be next door to the local call-house, a small boy was sitting and weeping.

'What's the matter, sonny?' asked a passer-by.

'Old Man Jones is loose,' he said. 'He killed three of the ladies in there, and now he's in our field chasing our heifers.'

44

THESE KIDS

The journalist was interviewing the record-breaking channel swimmer. 'How old are you?' he asked.

'Fifty-eight.'

'Fifty-eight and you just swam the channel! Incredible.'

'No, not in my family. My father's eighty, and he's a stunt man in Hollywood.'

'A stunt man!'

'And my grandfather is a hundred and five, and he's about to get married.'

'A hundred and five and he wants to get married!'

'No, no. He doesn't want to, he has to.'

EXCUSES, EXCUSES

An eighty-five-year-old couple get married. They have an elaborate wedding and then set off on a luxury cruise. After a candle-lit dinner with the best foods, the best wines and the best music, they go to the best cabin, theirs for the honeymoon. They get into bed.

The old man reaches over and takes her hand. 'Good night, dear.'

'Good night, dear,' she replies.

The next day they enjoy all that the ship has to offer, and again have a romantic dinner before they retire. He reaches over and takes her hand. 'Good night, dear.'

'Good night, dear.'

On the third day, the same sort of things happen. The dinner is more delicious than ever, the music more thrilling, the wine more inspiring. In their cabin he reaches over for her hand.

But she says, 'Not tonight, dear. I have a headache.'

HE LOST HIS MEMORY

An eighty-seven-year-old tells his friends, 'It isn't any fun to be old, because your memory always goes back on you.'

It seems he roused his wife that morning to have a little fun, but she said, 'Keep still, we did it twice not thirty minutes ago.'

He says, 'It's kind of sad when a man gets so old he can't remember things like that.'

THAT WILL BE DIFFERENT

Two old men are comparing notes. They agree, 'Taking it out is one thing, but putting it in is another.'

FIRE! FIRE!

In a row of houses the outdoor toilets were being dug up while new ones were already installed inside. Grandad was warned about the diggings by his children and grandchildren and reminded time and again that it was no longer necessary to leave the house.

But one night he forgot. He fell into you know what and started hollering 'Fire! Fire!'

The family ran and rescued him, hosed him down and dried him by the stove. They asked him, 'Why did you yell, "Fire! Fire?"! How was that going to save you? There wasn't any fire.'

He said, 'Well, you sure haven't got much sense. Did you ever hear of anybody being rescued hollering "Shit"?'
P.S.

Saint Bernard, when a youth, protected himself against an attempt upon his virtue by crying 'Thieves, thieves!' and so arousing the whole house.

(He obviously thought it no use to cry 'Buggery!' or 'Rape!' or even 'Fire!')

THE OLD WAY

A tutor was engaged for a young girl who was interested in sciences, and her grandmother was assigned to attend the lessons as chaperone.

One day the girl asked the teacher about the origin of man; how does it happen?

He replied that one takes the necessary elements in correct measures, mixes them, heats them, and after a certain time the man is made.

'Tell me, sir,' said the grandmother, 'the old way, is it altogether neglected?'

PERFECTLY LEGITIMATE

In Russia, the Cossacks used to raid the Jewish villages every so often. These attacks were called pogroms. The Cossacks would gallop up, kill the men and rape the women, take anything they fancied, and ride off again until the next time.

In one village, an old Jewish grandmother and her young grand-daughter were living by themselves. When the alarm went up that the Cossacks were coming, there was no way for them to escape. The best the grandmother could do was to hide the girl in a closet.

Sure enough, the door was beaten open, a Cossack came in, prodded the grandmother with his whip, and told her to lay down.

At this, the grand-daughter rushed out of the closet and cried, 'Take me, but spare my poor old grand-mother!'

This he duly did and went out. Hardly had he gone when another Cossack appeared. He nudged the grandmother with his boot. 'Lay down!'

Again the grand-daughter ran forward. 'Take me, but spare my poor old grandmother!'

He did, and went out. At that moment a third Cossack appeared. He pushed the old lady with his gun and said, 'Lay down!'

Once again the grand-daughter came forward. 'Take me, but spare my poor old grandmother!'

'Hush, darlink,' said the old woman. 'A pogrom is a pogrom!'

MODERN CHILDREN

On the first day of school, the children were sizing each other up and boasting.

One announced, 'I come from a one-parent family.'

Said another, '*I* come from a three-parent family!'

IN THE AMERICAN WEST

In the old days, two old men were arguing about which was senior, and they set out to prove it by who could remember farthest back.

They started out easy, like who could remember when he got his first tooth. Well, both could.

Then both could remember when they were born.

Finally one fellow says he can remember before he was born. Says his mother was setting out cabbage plants, and he remembers reaching out and pulling them up. 'Guess I was a real mean little devil in those days!'

The other old man thought for a couple of seconds, then he also remembered the time before he was born. Seems his Pa was on top of an Indian girl. 'It was my turn to be shot,' he said, 'but I reached up and grabbed my young brother by the legs, just to keep from going into that squaw. That's how close I come to being a goddamn Indian!'

The first old fellow didn't have no more to say.

PUNCH-UP

The police asked a little boy which of two men fighting in the street was his father.

'I don't rightly know. That's what they're fighting about.'

NOT YET

The fellows hanging around the local call-house noticed that the very old man who always came with a young chap hadn't turned up for two weeks. One of them saw him on the street and asked him about it – 'You finally giving up the girls, Grandpa?'

'No sirree! It's just that Jack's on holiday and so there's no one to put me on and lift me off.'

HIS COW

A deaf old man lost his cow. He lived at some distance from the village and he didn't attend church regularly any more, so when he happened to meet up with the preacher one day, he asked him to let folks know that she was missing. The preacher said he would.

The next Sunday evening, the old man thought he'd better show up in church. The preacher began talking about a young couple who were going to get married. He said the young lady was the cream of the crop and the flower of the flock and a fine example of Christian womanhood.

The old man understood that he was talking about his cow, though he couldn't quite make out what. But he stood up and hollered, 'And her rump's caved in, and she has one spoiled tit.'

There was a terrible fight. The sheriff grabbed the old man and rushed him to the jailhouse. He locked him up for his own good, and sneaked him back to his home the next day.

The old man said everyone in the village was a nut-case, and it wasn't safe for a respectable citizen to go there nowadays.

PRECOCIOUS

A little boy playing in the back garden gets angry and kicks a chicken. 'Just for that,' says his mother, 'you won't get any eggs for two weeks.'

Later the boy kicks a dog and is told that he will not get any hot dogs for two weeks.

The father comes home, drunk. He gets angry and kicks the cat.

'OK, Mum,' says the boy, 'are you going to tell him or shall I?'

FORTY YEARS AGO

A seventy-year-old woman confesses that she committed fornication forty years ago.

Somewhat surprised, the priest asks her why does she confess it now.

'It's so nice to recall it, Reverend Father!'

SAME FOR ALL?

One Sunday the preacher was exhorting the congregation with exceptional fervour.

'You are sinners headed into the fire and brimstone of Hell! The devil is rubbing his hands, waiting for you! Repent before it is too late, you who have been he-ing and she-ing! Repent! Pray to God and repent!'

Almost everyone started praying.

A small boy called from the back of the church, 'Reverend, how do you stand on me-ing and me-ing?'

HE RECOGNISES ME!

A recent widow kneels at her husband's grave, and the grass tickles her.

'Ah, he hasn't yet lost his amiable ways!'

A GALLANT MAN

At the market, two women who are selling vegetables from their stalls boast of their produce with gestures. One has two big onions and the other a very large carrot.

A deaf old woman seated nearby asks, 'Where does he live?'

FIRST SHE EVER SAW?

An old lady saw a whale spouting, and said, 'Tut, tut! It should quit laying on its back and showing off like that.'

SEVEN OLD LADIES

Oh dear, what can the matter be?
Seven old ladies were locked in the lavat'ry.
They were there from Monday 'til Saturday
And nobody knew they were there.

The first old lady was Mary Ann Porter,
She was the Deacon of Dorchester's daughter.
She went to relieve a slight pressure of water,
And nobody knew she was there.

The second old lady was Abigail Splatter,
She went there 'cause something was clearly the matter,
But when she got there, it was only her bladder,
And nobody knew she was there.

The third old lady was Amelia Garpickle,
Her urge was sincere, her reaction was fickle.
She jumped over the door; she'd forgotten her nickel,
And nobody knew she was there.

The fourth old lady was Hildegarde Foyle,
She hadn't been living according to Hoyle,
She was glad when the swelling was only a boil,
And nobody knew she was there.

The fifth old lady was Emily Clancy,
She went there 'cause something tickled her fancy,
But when she got there it was ants in her pantsy,
And nobody knew she was there.

The sixth old lady was extremely fertile,
Her name was O'Connor, the boys called her Myrtle.
She went there to repair a slight hole in her girdle,
And nobody knew she was there.

The seventh old lady was Barbara Bender,
She went there to repair a broken suspender.
It snapped up and ruined her feminine gender,
And nobody knew she was there.

The janitor came in the early morning.
He opened the door without any warning,
The seven old ladies their seats were adorning,
And nobody knew they were there.

SNAPOO

Oh madam, oh madam, your daughter's too fine –
  Snapoo!
Oh madam, oh madam, your daughter's too fine
To sleep with a soldier from over the Rhine –
  Snapoo!

Oh mother, oh mother, I'm not too fine –
  Snapoo!
Oh mother, oh mother, I'm not too fine
To sleep with a soldier from over the Rhine –
  Snapoo!

Oh mother, oh mother, he's teasing me –
  Snapoo!
Oh mother, oh mother, he's teasing me,
He's tickling the place for RSVP –
  Snapoo!

Oh mother, oh mother, he's on me yet –
  Snapoo!
Oh mother, oh mother, he's on me yet,
And if he don't stop he will surely beget –
  Snapoo!

Eight months rolled by and the ninth did pass –
  Snapoo!
Eight months rolled by and the ninth did pass,
And a little Dutch soldier marched out of the lass –
  Snapoo!

The little Dutch soldier he grew and grew –
  Snapoo!
The little Dutch soldier he grew and grew,
And now he's chasing the chippies too –
  Snapoo!

Wives

THE FIRST NIGHT

The bride was not a virgin, and she was worried about the first night.

'Don't worry, dear,' says her mother. 'Just put a cabbage leaf over yourself. Your husband will think it your maidenhead.'

She does this.

Next morning, the husband remarks, 'I came in with a cane and came out with an umbrella.'

SHE FLOATED UPSTREAM

They used to tell about the time old Jim Caldecott's wife fell into the river and drowned, and everybody came out to help find the corpse. They were dragging the bottom and the deep holes, and some folks were even shooting off dynamite below the bridge.

Pretty soon somebody saw old Jim poking around the weeds way up river from the place where she fell in. They thought he was just drunker than usual, and mixed up, but that wasn't it.

He figured that Lizzie was so contrary she wouldn't float downstream, even if she *was* dead.

SEASONAL

In a museum, the wife was eager to see the pictures in all the galleries, but her husband stood for a long time looking intently and closely at 'Spring'. This was a large oil painting of a beautiful girl dressed airily in one strategically arranged leaf.

'Come on!' exclaimed the wife impatiently. 'What are you waiting for? Autumn?'

EXPENSE STATEMENT

3/10	Ad for female stenographer	10.00
4/10	Violets for new stenographer	3.00
6/10	Week's salary for new stenographer	70.00
9/10	Roses for stenographer	10.00
10/10	Sweets for wife	1.00
13/10	Lunch for stenographer	17.00
15/10	Week's salary for stenographer	100.00
16/10	Film tickets for wife and self	2.50
18/10	Theatre tickets for steno and self	25.00
19/10	Ice cream for wife	.50
22/10	Mary's salary	125.00
23/10	Champagne & dinner for Mary and self	80.00
25/10	Doctor for stupid stenographer	575.00
26/10	Mink stole for wife	2,700.00
27/10	Ad for male stenographer	10.00

THE LINEN SHEET

A man going off on a long business trip asked his mother-in-law to move in with her daughter to keep her company. She agreed, and off he went.

Unknown to him, his wife was in love with another man. Now, she told her mother all about it. The mother indulged her daughter and encouraged the affair. They frequently invited the paramour to dinner.

One night while the three of them were eating, the husband unexpectedly returned. He rang the doorbell and called out that he was back. Imagine their upset! The wife hid her lover in another room, while the mother quickly washed off and put away the third plate and utensils. Then the daughter opened the door.

As soon as the husband came in, he asked them to get the bed ready as he was very tired and needed to rest. The wife didn't know what to do. Her mother, seeing this, said, 'Wait, don't get the bed ready until we have shown your husband the beautiful linen sheet we made while he was gone.'

And the old woman took out a linen sheet and held one end as high as she could, and signalling to her daughter, got her to hold up the other end. Behind the outspread sheet, the hidden lover was able to tiptoe away and escape. The husband, distracted by the sheet, saw nothing.

Then the mother said to the daughter, 'Spread this fine sheet that you and I made with our own hands on your husband's bed.'

He said to the old woman, 'And you, madam, know how to make such linen?'

She answered, 'My son, I have made many like this.'

SUSPICIONS

A business man was having an affair. His wife had been getting more and more suspicious, and finally one day she said as much to her maid.

'I think my husband is having an affair with his secretary.'

'Go on!' exclaimed the maid. 'You're only saying that to make me jealous!'

CONFESSIONS

On her deathbed, a wife calls for her husband.

She weeps as she tells him he was always so good to her, and she thanks him for everything. Then, between heart-broken sobs, she begs his forgiveness because – sob, sob – because over the years she had many, many lovers!

'That's why I poisoned you, honey.'

RECOGNITION

A man in a pub was suffering from the night before. He leaned on the counter and said to the barman, 'Give me something for a hangover.'

'What do you want?'

'Something tall, cold, and full of gin,' was the reply.

A drunk standing next to him lurched around. 'Take that back before I hit you!' he shouted. 'You are referring to the woman I married!'

IN SCOTLAND

A husband found his wife in another man's arms.

'Stand behind your lover, ye false woman!' he screamed. 'I'm going to shoot ye both!'

CUCKOLDED, BEATEN, AND HAPPY

In love at first sight with the beautiful wife of a rich old merchant, a handsome youth sold all his possessions and managed to get hired by the rich man. In this way he could see his beloved every day.

He was so diligent and proficient that he soon was the merchant's deputy, and before long he was able to speak of his love to the wife, who assured him that she loved him as well.

'You know which side of the bed I sleep on,' she said. 'Come to me tonight at midnight.'

At the stroke of the clock he came. It was completely dark. The merchant was asleep on the far side of the bed, but the lady was awake. She took the youth's hand in both of hers and held it tight. Then, 'Husband!' she cried.

Horrified, the youth tried to break away but could not. 'Husband, I meant to tell you earlier. Who is your favourite and most trusted employee?'

In the dark the frightened young man tugged and tugged to get loose, but she held on too closely.

'The new young man, my deputy,' said the husband.

'So I thought,' she replied. 'Well, do you know, this evening he proposed that I should meet him at the pine tree in the garden after midnight. This shows how much you can trust him!'

The terrified youth, no matter how he pulled and twisted, could not get free.

'Husband,' the wife continued, 'you must trap him. Put on one of my skirts and my veil, and go down to the garden and wait for him. He's bound to turn up, I'm sure of it.'

'Very well,' said the husband. 'I really should look into this.' So he stumbled about in the dark, found a skirt and a veil and went off to the garden.

When he was gone, the lady bolted the door from the inside. The young man by now understood what she had been up to and was overjoyed. They fell into each other's arms and had a delightful time together.

Presently she told him to dress. 'Darling,' she said, 'find a stick and go down to the garden. Pretend that you think my husband is me, and give him a good beating.'

The lover did just this, calling the merchant a shameless hussy. 'You thought I would wrong your husband, did you? I'll teach you! Take that, and that!'

Eventually the husband stumbled back to the bedroom. He was battered but happy. 'You see!' he said triumphantly to his wife, 'He had no intention of dishonouring me. He simply wanted to put you to the test.'

'We must reward his devotion,' said the wife.

And so he did. And she did.

FAIR QUESTION

'Charlie asked me to marry him, and make him the happiest man in the world.'

'And which did you decide to do?'

FIDDLED!

In port for a few days, the captain of a ship saw a pretty woman and was quite taken with her. He found out that she was married to a fiddler.

He went to the pub where the fiddler hung out, bought him some drinks, and told him he'd bet his ship against the other fellow's fiddle that he could seduce his wife in two hours.

'Not my wife!' cried the fiddler. 'She'd never consent.'

'Are you willing to bet, then?'

'I am.'

So the captain was given two hours in the fiddler's house with his wife.

The fiddler decided to go home to hear what was going on from outside the closed door. By the time he got there, there were some noises that sounded suspicious, so he sang out

Be true to me, be true to me,
Be true, my love, be true.
Be true to me till the clock strikes three,
And the ship belongs to you.

She sang out in reply

Too late, too late, my own true love,
He's got me round the middle.
He's got me once, he's got me twice,
And you've lost your damned old fiddle!

ALL IS FAIR

A wife had a lover unknown to her husband. The one thing she wanted was a fur coat, and the lover was eager to give it to her. The problem was this: how could she suddenly acquire a fur coat without her husband becoming suspicious?

At last they hit on the idea of his buying the coat and leaving it in a locker at Liverpool Street station. He would then give her the key, which she would pretend she had found on the street.

All went according to plan. One day she said to her husband, 'Darling, look what I found! A key to one of the lockers at Liverpool Street.'

'So what?' said he.

'Why don't you go down and claim whatever is in it?'

He said it wasn't honest and anyhow it was out of his way, but eventually he agreed to go there on his way to work and bring back with him that night whatever was in the locker.

He went to Liverpool Street, got the coat, and brought it to the office with him. He threw it down over a table, and his secretary came in and saw it.

'Darling!' she cried, and kissed him. 'Is this for me? After all these years? How wonderful!'

'Why – er – of course, of course. Sure it's for you. I just bought it.'

She was overjoyed.

That night his wife met him at the door, all excited. 'What was in the locker? Where is it?'

'Here,' he said, and handed her a second-hand umbrella he had bought in a pawn-shop on the way home.

TO MY EVERLOVING WIFE

To my dearest wife,

During the past year, I attempted to make love to you on 365 individual nights. I succeeded 36 times. This averages once every ten nights. The following is a list of the reasons you yourself gave me on the nights when I didn't succeed.

The children aren't asleep yet	3
We will wake the children	4
It's too hot	11
It's too cold	9
It's too late	16
It's too early	23
Pretending sleep	56
Window open – neighbours will hear	9
Backache	16
Toothache	2
Headache	10
Giggles	4
I'm too full	4
Not in the mood	21
Baby crying	19
Watched late show	7
Watched early show	5
Mud pack	2
Grease on face	1
Reading Sunday paper	48
Company in next room	7
You're too drunk	5
I'm too drunk	14

Do you think we could improve our record this coming year?

Your loving husband.

QUEUE

Husband: I don't know what's come over my wife. She suddenly rations me to two nights a week! What do you make of that?

Friend: Don't complain. I've heard that she's cut out some of the fellows altogether.

EMERGENCY?

The new maid seemed to be a real find. The wife and she had agreed on hours, pay and time off.

Then the wife said, 'Oh, one thing. After dinner, my husband sometimes asks for an unexpected treat. Would you be prepared for such an emergency?'

'Sure, that's all right, ma'am. I'm on the pill.'

GOLF

Two golfers were being held up by two women playing ahead of them. Finally one of the men said he would go forward and ask the ladies to give way.

Off he went. Minutes later he came back, very disturbed.

'One of them is my wife,' he said, 'and the other is my mistress! You'll have to speak to them.'

The other man went forward to do this. He was back minutes later.

'What a coincidence,' he said.

GET UP AND BAR THE DOOR

There lived a man in yonder glen,
   And John Blunt was his name, O.
He makes good malt and he brews good ale,
   And he bears a wondrous fame, O.

The wind blew in the hall one night,
   Full quick out o'er the moor.
'Rise up, rise up, old Lucy,' he says,
   'Rise up and bar the door.'

They made a paction tween them both,
   They made it firm and sure,
Whoeer should speak the foremost word,
   Should rise and bar the door.

Three travellers that had slowed their pace
   As through the hills they fore,
They sighted by the line of light
   Full straight for John Blunt's door.

They hurled old Lucy out of her bed
   And laid her on the floor,
But never a word would Lucy say
   For barring of the door.

'Ye've eaten my bread, ye've drunken my ale,
   And ye'll make my old wife a whore!'
'Aha, Johnnie Blunt! ye has spoke the first word,
   Get up and bar the door!'

NO BALLS AT ALL

Oh listen, my children
A story you'll hear,
A song I will sing you,
Twill fill you with cheer.

Chorus:
  No balls at all.
  No balls at all.
  Imagine a man
  Who had no balls at all.

A charming young maiden
Was wed in the fall.
She married a man
Who had no balls at all.

'Oh mother, oh mother,
Oh what shall I do?
I've married a man
Who's unable to screw.

For many long years
I've avoided the call,
Now I've married a man
Who has no balls at all.'

'Oh daughter, oh daughter,
Now don't feel so sad.
I had the same trouble
With your dear old Dad.

There are lots of young men
Who will answer the call
Of the wife of a man
Who has no balls at all.'

Now the daughter she followed
Her mother's advice.
And she found the proceedings
Exceedingly nice.

And a bouncing young baby
Was born in the fall,
To the wife of the man
Who had no balls at all.

Priests

COMPLETING THE JOB

While her husband was away, the curate convinced a pregnant wife that the expected child was imperfect because when it was conceived, the husband neglected to make the ears. He told her that this defect must be remedied without delay, and in her husband's absence offered to do the remedial work himself.

On the husband's return, the simple woman told him all about this good deed. The husband kept his anger to himself and bided his time. Not long afterward he had his revenge by cutting the ears off all the curate's pigs.

The curate was furious and complained about this outrage in church. Who did it?

Before the whole congregation the husband asked, 'Why are you so upset? Surely, anyone who can make ears on babies can do it to his pigs?'

PARROT

The parish priest is proudly showing off his pet parrot to the Archbishop. 'If you pull the string on his right leg, he recites the Lord's Prayer.'

He pulls the string and the parrot recites it.

'And if you pull the string on his left leg, he says the Credo.' And this too is demonstrated.

The Archbishop asks, 'What if you pull both the strings at the same time?'

The parrot replies, 'I'll fall off my perch, you dumb queer!'

SPOKEN FROM THE HEART

In Ireland, an old woman went to Mass as usual on Sunday. A new young priest was preaching about marriage.

When she came out, she said to her friend, 'I wish to God I knew as little about it as he does.'

A NEW KIND

During the war a pilot was shot down over occupied France. He parachuted safely and was secretly given refuge in an enclosed convent by the nuns, who dressed him as one of them.

After some time, a nun was seen to be pregnant. Hoping to keep the whole matter as quiet as possible, the Mother Superior decided that she must inspect all the nuns to find which was the masquerading man.

The pilot hoped to escape discovery by tying himself down. But when his turn.came and she inspected him, the string broke. Her spectacles were knocked off and they landed on his tool.

'Well, I've seen a lot in my time,' she exclaimed, 'but *never* one wearing glasses!'

FAITH REWARDED

It used to be considered a very bad omen if the first person one met in the morning was a priest.

Early one day a woman saw a priest walking toward her. She quickly crossed herself so no misfortune would occur. The priest noticed this, and when he came up to her he asked if she believed that something worse would happen because she had met him.

'I fear so,' she replied.

He said, 'It will be as you believe,' and threw her into a muddy ditch.

UNANIMOUS

A certain preacher was famous for his strong views about adultery. He thundered from the pulpit, 'This sin is so grave, I would prefer ten virgins to one married woman!'

And many of those present shared his opinion.

THE CONFESSIONAL AGAIN

At confession, a girl is out to trick the priest. She tells him she had to fit trousers for a man, because she is a seamstress.

'Very well', says the priest. 'I absolve you. Just bring me a pot of butter.'

The next day she brings a pot and leaves it in the vestibule. The priest later sees her departing and runs after her. 'What do you mean?' he cries. 'The pot had nothing in it!'

'Neither did the trousers!'

TRUTH CONFESSED

A curate in eastern Europe liked to have a jig or two with a willing woman. So he kept a pair of panties hanging on the confessional.

His method was to say to each female who entered, 'Take down the panties.'

If one took off her own, she was loose and he had his fun with her. An honest woman would take down the hanging one.

JOINING THE MONKS

A youth on a Greek island is thinking of joining a monastery and goes to look one over. He is shown through many corridors, many rooms and many cells. He sees monks masturbating, practising sodomy, and finally comes on three monks in a row, having at each other from the rear.

Then he is brought to meet the abbot. He tells him that after what he has seen, he doesn't want to become a monk.

'Ah, my son,' says the abbot, 'don't be hasty. You must have patience. After three years, *you*'ll get to be the man in the middle!'

FORCE OF THE HABIT

A parish priest was very poor, and so he was dismayed when his bishop announced he was coming for a visit. There was only one bed, so as long as the bishop would be staying, the priest's housekeeper was going to have to sleep on the floor.

Things went pretty well during the day, and in the night the bishop and the priest retired to bed. But in the early morning, the priest was awakened as usual by the milk delivery. He slapped the bishop twice on the backside and said, 'Get up, Mary, and get the breakfast.'

CONFESSIONAL

In confession, a girl told the priest that she had had intercourse with a man.

'Was it against your wishes?' he asked.

'No, Father, it was against the china closet, and it would do your heart good to hear the dishes rattling!'

CONFESSIONAL AGAIN

Two girls go to the priest together. The first girl as penance has to keep her hand in holy water for two hours, because she had put it in a boy's pants.

The second girl has to sit for two hours in the font.

AND AGAIN

A man told his confessor that he'd had at it with his cat, and that it was better than with a woman.

'How did you do it?'

'I took him by the front paws and went right in.'

Later, the man came back again and confessed the same sin.

'It's a lie!' cried the priest. 'I tried, and got scratched.' He closed the confessional.

THE PEASANT'S COW

Because the priest tells his flock that whatever you give in God's name will be returned to you multiplied, the peasant gives him his only cow. And sure enough, in a few days she comes back to the peasant's yard leading the priest's cows after her.

The peasant takes this as God's doing, but the priest claims they are his. They finally agree that the cows will go to whoever is first to say good-morning to the other on the next day.

To be sure to be first, the peasant that night climbs a tree next to the priest's house. Thus he happens to hear and see the priest and his servant go to bed together, and learns that what she has is called Rome and what he has is called the Pope. After this lesson the peasant goes to sleep in the tree.

First thing the next morning, he hails the priest from his perch.

The priest asks, 'How long have you been in that tree?'

'Since the Pope entered Rome.'

'Enough. The cows are yours.'

FISH

The congregation always brought their gifts to the vicar on Sunday morning before the service. One of the gifts this Sunday was a live fish. The vicar had nothing to put it in nor even to wrap it in, so he tied it to his belt underneath his vestments.

During the sermon the fish started to leap about, and the people in the church started to laugh.

'My children,' cried the vicar, 'you are in error! You think it's flesh, but it's fish!'

THE PRIEST'S DOG

The priest believed his dog was very smart. His sacristan said he had heard of an academy where they could teach dogs to speak. Would the priest like him to bring the dog there and enrol him?

The priest was delighted. Actually, the sacristan took the dog and did away with him.

When the time came for the course to be over, the priest sent the sacristan off with the fairly costly payment and waited eagerly for the dog's return. The sacristan, however, simply pocketed the money and returned alone.

'Where is my dog?' cried the priest.

'I had to drown him.'

'Oh no! My poor dog! Why did you do such a dreadful act?'

'The school was excellent, Father, and the dog learned to speak very well. But the first thing he asked me was if you were still sleeping with the maid. So I had no choice.'

Sadly the priest approved.

CANONISED

A Queen of France after several years of marriage was still without a child. She decided to make a pilgrimage to Chartres to pray in the cathedral there.

Along the route many country people had gathered to show their respect and to follow her. 'May your Majesty have many children!' they called to her. Others cheered, 'May your trip to Chartres be blessed!'

But one old woman cried out, 'Don't go there. The canon who made them there is dead.'

HANGING

A friar was famous for his fiery sermons of sympathy for martyrs and others who died for their faith. 'When Saint Stephen's Day is celebrated,' he would cry, 'I feel the arrows that killed him!'

He was also well-known for his preaching on the necessity to speak plainly. 'Don't mince words,' he said. 'Call everything by its proper name, in innocence or in anger.'

Once he was praising a fellow friar who had been hanged, and the folk in church thought he himself was either innocent or angry when he proclaimed, 'I hang as well as he!'

MORE HANGING

At a Rural Electricity Station in Ireland, one of the workmen caused a lot of trouble by seducing – one after the other – the girls who also worked at the station. After hours, on the tops of the office desks, so it was said.

Eventually there were so many fights, beatings and general mayhem in the place that work was seriously affected. The supervisor could get nowhere. Finally he decided to ask the parish priest to speak to the culprit.

The priest called him in, told him what he'd heard, and asked if it were true.

'It is, Father, it is.'

'You can stand there in front of me and say that shamelessly! Without any remorse for the grief you've caused, ruining the lives of those unfortunate women, to say nothing of their husbands and families! How could you do it?'

'I guess it's because I'm well-hung.'

THE NEW PRIEST

At confession, the new young priest can't figure out the fractions for sins and penance. He hears the bishop tell a man with seven sins that he should say three Paters and two Aves.

So at last he says to his communicant, 'Go and do it twice more and then come back tomorrow.'

LOCAL DIALECT

A young curate from town was sent to be the new village priest when the old priest died. As he started on his work, his main concern was to get to know his flock well, and in order to do this he fixed two days of contrition, Saturdays for men and the following Wednesdays for the women.

When the Saturdays came round, the priest noticed to his surprise that the young lads had very few sins. After he encouraged them to tell all, one for example would say, 'I played bowls on Whitsun.' Then another would say the same. A third would say that he played bowls on All Souls.

'That's no sin,' the priest said to each, and he remained puzzled. But he suddenly saw light on the Wednesdays, when the young women, asked to confess serious sins, replied, 'I allowed bowling on Whit Monday', or 'I allowed bowling on All Souls.'

BOWLING AGAIN

But then there is the one about a young prince who was a suitor for the hand of a beautiful princess. She was famous as an athlete, and her father the king had laid down the conditions for winning her.

She would be anointed with oil and then stark naked would run ahead of any suitor. The one who could catch her and hold on to her would win her. Many young men had tried to do this; some had caught up with her and even caught her, but because of the slippery oil, none could hold her.

What to do?

The prince summoned his advisors. They could not think of any stratagem, and finally an old priest was called in.

He simply asked, 'Do you bowl, Sire?'

RESPECT NOT NEEDED

There were at one time strapping women porters in Belgium, as strong and as rough as the men. One of them was relieving herself in an alley when a priest passed by. She went to stand up.

'Stay, my daughter,' he said. 'I'd rather see the hen than the egg.'

THE FRIAR IN THE WELL

As I lay musing all alone, fa, la, la, la
A pretty jest I thought upon, fa, la, la, la, la
Then listen a while, and I will you tell
Of a friar that loved a bonny lass well.
Fa, la, la, la, la, fa, la, la, lang-tre-down-dilly.

He came to the maid when she went to bed,
Desiring to have her maidenhead.
But she denied him his desire,
And told him that she feared hell-fire.

'Tush,' quoth the friar, 'thou needst not doubt
If thou wert in hell I could sing thee out.'
'Then,' quoth the maid, 'thou shalt have thy request.'
The friar was as glad as fox in his nest.

'But one thing,' quoth she, 'I do desire,
Before you have what you require,
Before that you shall do the thing,
An angel of money thou shalt me bring.'

'Tush,' quoth the friar, 'we shall agree,
No money shall part my love and me.
Before that I will see thee lack,
I'll pawn the grey gown from my back.'

The maid bethought her of a wile.
How she the friar might beguile.
While he was gone, the truth to tell,
She hung a cloth before the well.

The friar came, as his covenant was,
With money to his bonny lass,
'Good morrow, fair maid!' 'Good morrow!' quoth she.
'Here is the money I promised thee.'

She thanked the man, and she took his money.
'Now let us go to it,' quoth he, 'sweet honey.'
'O stay,' quoth she, 'some respite make,
My father comes, he will me take.'

'Alas!' quoth the friar, 'where shall I run,
To hide me till that he be gone?'
'Behind the cloth run thou,' quoth she,
'And there my father cannot thee see.'

Behind the cloth the friar crept,
And into the well on the sudden he lept.
'Alas,' quoth he, 'I am in the well!'
'No matter,' quoth she, 'if thou wert in hell.

Thou sayst thou couldst sing me out of hell,
Now prithee sing thyself out of the well.'
The friar sung with a pitiful sound,
'Oh help me out, or I shall be drowned!'

Quoth he, 'For sweet Saint Francis' sake
On his disciple some pity take.'
Quoth she, 'Saint Francis never taught
His scholars to tempt young maids to naught.'

The friar did entreat her still
That she should help him out of the well.
She heard him make such piteous moan
She helped him out and bid him be gone.

Quoth he, 'Shall I have my money again,
Which thou from me hast beforehand tane?'
'Good sir,' said she, 'there's no such matter.
I'll make you pay for fouling my water.'

The friar went all along the street,
Dripping wet like a new-washed sheep.
Both old and young commended the maid
That such a witty prank had played.

A MIRACLE

A hermit once lived in a beautiful dell,
And it is no legend that I now tell,
So my father declared, who knew him quite well,
   The hermit.

He lived in a cave by the side of the lake,
Decoctions of herbs for his health he would take,
And only of fish could this good man partake,
   On Friday.

And most of this time he spent in repose,
Once a year he would bathe, both his body and clothes,
How the lake ever stood it, the Lord only knows,
   And he won't tell.

One day as he rose, dripping and wet,
His horrified vision three pretty girls met.
In matters of gallantry he wasn't a vet,
   So he blushed.

He grabbed up his hat that lay on the beach,
And covered up all that its wide brim would reach,
Then he cried to the girls in a horrified screech,
   'Go away!'

But the girls only laughed at his pitiful plight,
And begged him to show them the wonderful sight,
But he clung to his hat with all of his might,
   To hide it.

But just at this moment a villainous gnat
Made the hermit forget just where he was at,
He struck at the insect and let go the hat –
   Oh horrors!

Now I have come to the thread of my tale;
At first he turned red, and then he grew pale,
Then he uttered a prayer for prayers never fail,
    So 'tis said.

Of the truth of this tale, there is no doubt at all;
The Lord heard his prayer and answered his call.
Though he let go the hat, the hat didn't fall.
    Miracle!

Reverends

HALLELUIAH

On a barnstorming tour, a revivalist preacher was having great success packing in the crowds. Not only were there more conversions than ever before, but more people came along for the first time.

At one meeting a big fat woman got religion. She pranced down the aisle shouting, 'Revelation! Revelation! Halleluiah!', until, right up on the platform, she fell. Her skirts came up over her head, and the revelation was that she was wearing no pants.

One of the newcomers rushed up and tried to pull her clothes back over, but the preacher wouldn't have it.

'Halleluiah!' he cried. 'Let her lie how Jesus flang her!'

HALLELUIAH, BUM AGAIN

At Christmas time, the minister was staging a miracle play in which his housekeeper, all dressed up with wings, took the part of the Holy Ghost. But something went wrong with the flooring, and the Holy Ghost fell upside down into a hole.

The minister called out, 'Don't look, dear brothers, don't look! You will go blind!'

An old hunchback said, 'I'll risk one eye.'

FRIENDLY, ANYHOW

The old lady was about ninety years old. One day she didn't feel well, so the family sent to town for a doctor.

After he left, the old lady said, 'It was very nice of that new preacher to come.'

Her daughter said, 'Why mother, that wasn't a preacher, that was a doctor.'

The old lady looked a little taken aback. 'Oh. That explains it. I *thought* he acted kind of familiar, for a preacher.'

IN SCOTLAND

A dissatisfied bride complains to the womenfolk in church that her husband's is too small and she wants a divorce.

After full consideration of the complaint, the women agree to examine the matter. They decide that the husband is to stand behind a screen and show it through a hole in the screen.

Justifiably worried, he consults the minister, and the minister agrees to substitute for him.

The women file past the screen and one by one they are amazed. They say that instead of complaining, that hussy should give thanks unto the Lord, and no divorce for her!

Just then one of the matrons cries out. 'That's not her husband's, that's the minister's! I ken't by the wart o' the point o't.'

CONCLUSIVE

An elder of the church was called up before the bishops because he was supposed to have made his wife leave a church meeting.

He said: 'First, I never try to influence my wife. Second, my wife did not attend the meeting. Third, I did not attend the meeting. Fourth, neither my wife nor myself had any inclination to go to the meeting. And finally, gentlemen, I've never had a wife.'

NEW MANAGEMENT

The new vicar, never before married, became the husband of his predecessor's widow. On the wedding night he asked her to kneel with him beside the bed while he prayed aloud. He ended with, 'Oh Lord, give me strength and direction.'

'Just ask for strength,' said the bride. 'I'll take care of the directing.'

VICARIOUS

Two vicars were sitting on a park bench, doing their crossword puzzle, a regular custom of theirs.

First vicar (very agitated): Tut tut! Oh, tut tut!

Second vicar: Is anything the matter, vicar?

First vicar: Oh dear, yes. It's this crossword puzzle. It's really most embarrassing!

Second vicar: Well, let me help.

First vicar: It's the second clue down. A four-letter word that ends with U, N, T, and the clue is 'essentially feminine'.

Second vicar: U N T, U N T. Mmm. Essentially feminine, you say? Aha, I know! That will be 'aunt'.

First vicar: Aunt? – Oh yes, I see. Aunt. Er, you don't have a rubber I could borrow, do you?'

MISSIONARY

A widow-woman came to town, and she played havoc with the men. The women-folk wanted her to be put in jail, but the men thought that would be too hard on her. Finally the elders of the church were consulted, and they commissioned the preacher to visit her and persuade her to leave.

So one of the fellows who knew the way drove the preacher to her house. He waited outside, because the preacher had said he'd be back in a few minutes. Instead, a long time passed. Finally the preacher came out.

'You know, Jim,' he said, 'they've got it all wrong. That widow is a good Christian woman!'

'All right, Reverend,' said Jim. 'Just zip up your pants, and we'll get home in time for dinner.'

A GOOD DOSE

A boy walked into a call-house and told the Madam that he wanted a good dose of clap.

She could hardly believe her ears. 'You don't know what you're talking about! What do you want with that?'

'So I can give it to Sis.'

'To your sister? You can't mean that! What did your sister do to you?'

'Sis?' said the boy, very surprised. 'She never did anything. But she'll give it to Pa in a couple of days.'

'Good Lord! What do you have against your father then?'

The boy just looked at her, puzzled. 'Pa's all right. I just want him to give Ma a good dose.'

The woman was now horrified. 'It's a terrible thing for a boy to hate his own mother!'

'Why, I haven't got anything against Ma.'

'You haven't? Then why do you want her to get the clap?'

'Well,' he said, 'she'll give it to that goddamn preacher that put me out of Sunday School. He's the son-of-a-bitch I'm after!'

HE THANKED HIM

Right in the middle of a sermon, a man jumped up and ran out of the church. No one knew what to make of it.

But the next day he came to see the parson. He thanked him for the sermon. 'About a week ago I lost my umbrella. When you came to the part about thou shalt not commit adultery, all of a sudden I remembered where I'd left it.'

NONDENOMINATIONAL

A priest, a Protestant clergyman, and a rabbi occasionally met to gamble together in an unlicensed premises.

As luck would have it, one evening a policeman came in and arrested them. They were brought before a magistrate.

He said to the priest, 'You are accused of gambling. What have you to say?'

The priest looked up at heaven, gave a quick wink, and silently prayed. 'Oh God, a little white lie. OK? Then I'll never do it again.' He said out loud, 'Not guilty.'

The magistrate said, 'Very well, you can go.'

Then the clergyman was brought before him. 'You are accused of gambling,' said the magistrate. 'What have you to say?'

The clergyman looked up at heaven for a moment, then bowed his head and silently prayed. 'Oh God, just a little white lie, this once. I'll never do it again.' Out loud he said, 'Not guilty.'

The magistrate said, 'You can go.'

The rabbi was brought forward next. 'You are accused of gambling. What have you to say?'

The rabbi replied, 'Gambling? Who with?'

THE FIRE SHIP

As I stepped out one evening
Upon a night's career,
I spied a lofty clipper-ship
And after her I steered.
I hoisted up my sig-in-als
Which she so quickly knew,
And when she saw my sig-in-als fly,
She immediately hove to.

Chorus:
   She had a dark and a roving eye,
   And her hair hung down in ring-a-lets.
   She was a nice girl, a decent girl,
   But one of the rakish kind.

'Oh sailor, please excuse me
For being out so late.
For if my parents knew of it,
Oh, sad would be my fate!
My father is a minister,
A good and righteous man.
My mother is a Methodist,
So I do the best I can.'

I eyed that girl both up and down
For I'd heard such talk before.
And when she moored herself to me,
I knew she wanted more.
But still she was a pretty girl,
She shyly hung her head.
'I'll go along with you, my lad,'
This to me she said.

I took her to a nice hotel,
I knew she wouldn't mind.
But little did I think that she
Was one of the rakish kind.
I played with her for quite some time
And learned to my surprise,
She was nothing but a fire-ship
Dressed up in a disguise.

Then in the morning she was gone.
My money was gone too.
My clothes she'd hocked, my watch she stole,
My sea bag was done too.
But she left behind a souvenir
I'd have you all to know.
And in nine days, to my surprise,
There was fire down below.

Professions and Trades

ABSENT-MINDED PROFESSOR

Professor Johnson's family was moving house. Knowing how forgetful her husband could be, his wife put a slip of paper in each of his pockets with the new address written on it. When his classes were over, all he had to do was to take out one of the slips and then drive to his new home.

But during the course of the day, he used every single piece of paper to write notes on, and then gave the notes to his students. Work over, he got into his car. It was then that he suddenly remembered that this was moving day.

He could not recall at all where he was to go. But he had an inspiration. He drove to his old house, and luckily enough, there were some children playing outside.

'Hi little girl!' he called to a child who was near. 'Can you tell me where the Johnsons have moved to?'

'Sure. It's just around the corner and two houses down – Daddy.'

AND ANOTHER

At a formal dinner, an absent-minded professor sat next to a charming woman.

'Don't you remember me, Professor?' she asked. 'Some years ago you asked me to marry you.'

'Ah yes!' said the professor. 'And did you?'

NEVER FORGETS A FACE

A woman comes into a V.D. clinic. 'Don't you remember me, doctor? I used to come to your clinic in Birmingham.'

'No, I don't.'

But a few minutes later, when she is on the examining table, 'Oh, I remember you.'

DOCTORS AGAIN

A man said that his wife made too much fuss over having a baby, which, he said, didn't hurt any more than getting rid of a tapeworm.

'All right,' she said, 'I'll fix it with the doctor for you to have our next baby.'

Next time he got drunk they put him to bed, gave him some oil and plastered up his backside, and next morning he was swelled up like a balloon and bawling like a banshee. The doctor hid a little monkey in the bed, and then cut the plaster loose.

The man let out a bellow and the bed was running! The poor monkey was wiping the stuff out of his eyes and chattering and jumping around. When he saw it, the man yelled, 'What does the little bastard mean, laughing like a fool when his poor mother is a-dying?'

Once they got the place cleaned up, and him sobered up, they persuaded him that he dreamed the whole thing, and the doctor told him to go easy on the drink. He never made cracks again about having a baby.

HEAT RISING

A husband unexpectedly came home while a doctor was attending his sick wife and found them in bed together.

'What the devil's going on here?'

'Er – I'm taking your wife's temperature!'

'All right, but that thing better have numbers on it when you take it out.'

CURE

In the past, a country hospital somehow got filled up with squatters, instead of the sick and the old. The religious order which ran it was hard put to make ends meet and was thinking of closing.

A clever countryman who heard of this problem went to the bishop and offered to solve it. He then dressed like a doctor and visited the hospital. He was announced as a famous specialist, and the patients were called together to be examined by this great man.

He looked at them all and then addressed them.

'There is one remedy which will heal every one of you,' he announced. 'Whoever is the sickest will be brought forward. He will then be burned outside there in the square, and his ashes, as you will see, will cure the rest of you. Now, which of you is the sickest, please?'

Each patient declared that he had been miraculously cured and was not sick at all, not in the least! They were all 'allowed' to go home.

CONDITION IMPROVED

An old lady wasn't feeling well. She went to the doctor, who gave her medicine and told her to keep track of what passed. By the next day she was feeling a little better.

'Did anything out of the ordinary pass?'

'No, just a big lorry, a load of hay, and two foreigners on motorcycles.'

'Well,' he said, 'it's no wonder you're feeling better.'

EMERGENCY

A girl was too vain to wear glasses, but she always managed to conceal completely the fact that she was very, very shortsighted.

In due course she got married and went off with her husband on their honeymoon.

When she got back, her mother shrieked and ran to the telephone. She called an oculist.

'Doctor, come over here right away! It's an emergency. My daughter has always refused to wear glasses and now she's back from her honeymoon and –'

The doctor interrupted her. 'Madam, please calm yourself! Ask your daughter to come to see me. No matter how bad her eyes are, it can't be that much of an emergency.'

'Oh no?' screamed the mother. 'Well, this fellow she's got with her isn't the one she went on honeymoon with!'

NOT ASKING MUCH

An old man was sure he was going to die. He went to the doctor.

But the doctor couldn't find anything the matter. 'There's nothing to be done,' he said. 'I can't make people young again.'

The old man explained. 'Doctor, I don't want to be young again. All I want is to get a few years older!'

IF:

A hat-factory girl gets felt three times a day and
A fishmonger displays his cod every morning and
A baker rolls his dough every night and
A miller gets his oats three times a week and
A builder puts up some sort of an erection every three months and
A jockey gets a ride every Saturday and
A dustman hauls his ashes once a week
Why the HELL should a doctor get £25 for coming once?

THE LAWYER

A pretty young girl presented to a lawyer a petition against a man who had seduced her.

The lawyer didn't take the time to read it but proceeded to seduce her himself. 'Did he do this?'

'Yes, and more,' sobbed the girl.

Presently, 'And this?'

'Yes, and more!'

'This?'

'Yes, and more and more and more,' she sobbed.

Whatever the lawyer did, the girl still kept weeping, 'And more, and more!'

The seducer had apparently been able to start all over again, but the lawyer at last could not keep up.

'What more could he do?' he asked.

'Ah, sir, he gave me the clap!'

AND FROM MARK TWAIN

Mark Twain reported on a case of rape in Hartford, Connecticut. The defence lawyer, who was very small in stature, was questioning the complainant in court. She was a huge Irishwoman who testified that she had wakened in the morning and had found the accused lying beside her, and had discovered that she had been raped.

'Now, Madam,' sneered the lawyer, 'if one may take so preposterous a thing as that seriously, you might even charge it upon me. Come now, suppose you should wake up and find me lying beside you? What would you think?'

She measured him with her eyes critically and at her leisure, and said, 'I'd think I'd had a miscarriage.'

MORE RAPE

A small Negro boy is on trial in court, charged with rape. His mother is called up by the defence lawyer. She is very indignant that her son should be accused.

'Yo Honour,' she says, 'he's jes' too young! See fo yo'self, yo Honour,' opening the boy's fly, 'do you think this lil thing ah'm holding could do any harm?'

'Watch it, Mom,' says the boy. 'You better take yo warm hand off the evidence or we'll lose the case!'

A TEACHER

A Psychology teacher at the University was telling his friends about one of his classes. He had asked his students for a show of hands to explain the theory of psychosexual development, and only one student had volunteered.

'He explained,' said the teacher, 'how the first stage is the oral, and that in this there is interest in what goes into the mouth. This was correct, so I thought he should continue. "What is the next stage?" I asked him.'

' "The next stage is the anal," he said. "Interest here concentrates on what comes out as waste products." '

"Very good," I said. "And is there another stage?"

' "Yes," he said. "The third stage is the phallic. In this the interest is in the gentile area." '

'This was a very good answer,' said the teacher. 'And the funny part was, he wasn't Jewish. He was a genital.'

A TEACHER ADVISES

'Illiterate? Write today for Free Help Brochure.'

DEAFINITION

Lecturer – someone who talks in your sleep.

AT SCHOOL

The teacher comes into the classroom to find SHIT written on the blackboard.

'Now I'm not going to scold,' she says. 'We're going to take care of this on the honour system. We're all going to shut our eyes while I count out loud to a hundred, and when we open them I want that to be erased.'

They all close their eyes and she counts. Pitter-patter. Squeak-squeak. Pitter-patter. 'One hundred!'

They open their eyes and look. On the floor below the blackboard is a fresh pile of shit, and chalked above it, 'The Phantom strikes again!'

BAD BOY

In the morning, a mother finds her son still in bed when he should be leaving the house. 'Come on, get up! You must go to school.'

'I'm not going.'

'Yes, you are.'

'No, I'm not. I have my reasons.'

'All right. Give me two good reasons why you don't want to go.'

'Well, first, the children don't like me. And second, the teachers don't like me.'

'That makes no difference. You have to go anyway.'

'Then you give me two good reasons why I must!'

'Very well. First, you're forty-two years old. And second, you're the principal.'

FARMERS

At dinner at a Pennsylvania Dutch farmer's house, one of the children breaks wind noisily.

A guest asks, 'Do you allow the children to do this before you?'

'Vell,' says the farmer, 've haf no rules aboud it. Sometimes dem first, sometimes me first.'

FARMERS AGAIN

At a weekly market in France, a buyer looks over all the piglets that a farmer has for sale. According to him, there is something wrong with each of them.

The farmer waits until a crowd has gathered and then calls out to the buyer, 'I'll get the sow and you can *make* what you want.'

CENSUS-TAKER

The census-taker came to a run-down house where there was a woman and a flock of children. He asked the usual questions, and when he got to the children, she said that they all belonged to her.

'I'm only a poor woman that lives by taking in washing. I don't have a husband. I just have to get my children as best I can.'

AND ANOTHER

Census-taker (this time a woman): Married?
Woman: Yes ma'am, I been married twice.
Census-taker: Any children?
Woman: Six.
Census-taker: All by the same father?
Woman: No ma'am. I had two by my first husband, two by my second, and two by myself.

SOCIAL WORK

The social-worker called on a woman who had just lost
her husband, and found her in bed with another man.

'And your husband's been dead hardly a week!' she
exclaimed.

'Yessum. He's dead, not me.

AN OUNCE OF PREVENTION

Every time the doctor's wife goes away for a week, she
leaves seven apples on the maid's bed.

FORTUNE-TELLER

In a Jewish-American neighbourhood, a medium advertised for customers, so a woman went to the address and rang the doorbell. The medium came down.

'Can you talk vit the dead?' asked the woman.

'Can I talk vit the dead! Can a fish svim? I can do everythink – table-rappink, card-readink, fortune-tellink, astrology, dreams, crystal-ball, seance – caterink! Vat do you vant?'

'I vant to speak a few vords vit my grandmother who died in Gdansk.'

The medium brought her into a room, pulled down the blinds and turned off the lights. There was a breathless silence, then sounds of winds blowing. The medium went into a trance. Finally a voice was heard.

'This is your grandmother, darlink!'

'Oh grandmother, how is it by you?'

'It's lofly and beautiful here, dear.'

'How is Uncle Joe?'

'He's happy, so happy!'

Then there was a lot of noise like static. Some time passed before the voice came on again, and then it said, 'I must leave soon now, my dearest.'

'Oh grandmother, just von more question I vould like to esk!'

'Of course, darlink. Esk.'

'Vere the hell did you learn English?'

WORKMEN

Plumber: I remember your little boy, ma'm. He was in the infants' school when I went to do a job there.

Housewife: And what class was he in when you finished?

CHINESE DETECTIVE

A man suspected his beautiful wife of being a little friendly with another man. He therefore hired that famous Chinese detective, Wong Tang Pan, to watch and report any activities that might develop.

A few days later he received this report:

You leave
I watch house
He comes to house
I watch
He and she leave house
I follow
He and she get off train
I follow
He and she go in hotel
I climb tree and look in window.

He kiss she
She kiss he
He strip she
She strip he
He play with she
She play with he
I play with me
Fall out of tree
NO SEE – NO FEE

THE WRONG TRADE

An assistant in a clothing shop loves the boss's daughter. She promises him that he will be her first lover, even though she becomes engaged to a rich young man.

So on the wedding-night in all her wedding finery she runs to keep a tryst with the assistant in the garden. But he won't make love lest her dress be spoiled, and goes to fetch a carpet.

When he returns, she has changed her mind.

'Find a shop-girl!' she says. 'What you're a real master of is the dress trade!'

SIMPLE

If a girl with briefs is a lawyer, what is a girl without briefs?
A solicitor.

THE CHARLESTON MERCHANT

There was a wealthy merchant,
In Charleston he did dwell.
He had a pretty woman,
The tailor loved her well.

Chorus:
   Come a rotty trotty trotty
   A rotty trotty tree.

She met him on the highway,
And these words she did say,
'My husband's gone to sea,
So come and stay with me.'

He hadn't been there
But a quarter-hour or more,
When along come the merchant
A-knocking at the door.

It woke up that tailor
In the middle of his sleep,
Crying, 'Oh dear woman,
Whereto shall I creep?'

She went downstairs
For to open up the door,
And there stood her husband
And several others more.

She gave him a hug
And she gave him a kiss,
Saying, 'Oh dear husband,
What's the meaning of this?'

'I didn't come here
To disturb you of your rest.
I'm going off to sea
And I come to get my chest.'

Then in walked four men
Big and strong.
They lifted up the chest
And they toted it along.

They hadn't got more
Than a quarter-mile from town,
When the weight of the tailor
Made the sweat roll down.

They set the chest down
For to get a moment's rest.
Says one to the other,
'The Devil's in that chest!'

So they opened up the chest
Right there before them all.
And there lay the tailor
Like a piggy in the straw.

'If I don't drown you
Then hell damn me!
For I don't want you raising
Any tailor kids for me!'

So they locked him in the chest
And they threw him in the sea.
And that was the end
Of the little tailoree.

BELL-BOTTOM TROUSERS

When I was just a serving maid who lived in Drury Lane,
My master he was kind to me; my mistress was the same.
When along came a sailor boy with laugh so bright and free,
And he was the source of all my misery.

Chorus: With his bell-bottom trousers, suit of navy blue,
         He would climb the rigging like his daddy used to do.

He asked me for a candle to light him to his bed,
He asked me for a nightcap to put upon his head.
Now I was just a simple lass and didn't mean no harm,
So I hopped into the sailor's bed to keep the sailor warm.

In the morning he was gone and left a five-pound note,
With a bit of writing on it, and this is what he wrote:
'Now you may have a daughter, or you may have a son,
And this should help to pay for the trouble I have done.

Now if you have a daughter, you can bounce her on your knee,
But if you have a son, you can send him off to sea.
With his bell-bottom trousers, suit of navy blue,
He will climb the rigging like his daddy used to do.'

In the Country

THREE IN A BED

A travelling salesman asks to stay overnight with a farmer and his wife. He is very polite at supper, and the wife makes eyes at him. Afterwards all three share the one bed in the house.

In the middle of the night the barn catches fire, and the farmer throws on his clothes and runs out.

'Now's your chance!' says the wife.

So the salesman rushes downstairs and eats the rest of the beans.

SHE COULDN'T

An English soldier stayed overnight in a French peasant's cottage, sharing the bed of the old peasant and his young wife. In the middle of the night, some peculiar noises woke the husband.

'Psst!' he whispered to his wife. 'He is riding you! Tell him to keep quiet.'

'I can't,' she said. 'I don't know English.'

THE TRAVELLING SALESWOMAN

When night falls, the travelling saleslady stops at the only farmhouse in sight. There is no extra bed, so she must sleep with the farmer's son.

After a while she says to him, 'Let's trade sides. I'll roll under you and you roll over me.'

'Oh, that's all right, lady. I'll just get up and walk around the bed.'

She tries again and the same thing happens. And again. Finally she says to him, 'I don't think you know what I really want.'

'I sure do! You want the whole damn bed, but you ain't goin' to get it.'

COWS AND BULLS

An elderly couple are shown a bull at the county fair who has done his duty ten times a week. 'Hear that, Pa?' crows the old woman.

Another has done it fourteen times. 'Hear that, Pa?'

'But not to the same cow, was it?' asks the old man.

The attendant explains, 'Oh no, sir, it is a different cow each time.'

'Hear that, Ma?'

She had no more to say.

MORE BULL

One day the farmer has to go to market and his big son Fred is away, so he leaves his younger son in charge of the bull. He reminds him that a service costs ten pounds.

A neighbour comes along looking for the older brother.

'He ain't here.'

'I have to see him. You know what he done? He got my daughter pregnant!'

The boy says, 'You'll just have to wait till Pa comes home. I don't know what he charges for Fred.'

BULL

A prize bull was on display inside a special tent at a big fair. A father who had brought along all his fourteen children was wondering if he could afford to pay for them to go in.

'Listen,' said the ticket-seller, 'you and your family are all going in free. I want that bull to get a look at you.'

BULLS AND COWS

A boy was absent from school one day. The next day he explained to the teacher that he had had to take the cow to the bull.

'Surely that wasn't necessary,' she told him. 'Your father could have done it.'

'Oh no, ma'am,' cried the boy. 'It has to be a bull!'

COWS, BULLS AND HORSES

A city couple were being taken around a big farm. They saw the fields, the machinery, the milking-parlour, the hen-houses, the pig houses, the stables and the different livestock.

Of all this, the wife was most impressed by the bull, who while they watched, serviced three cows in succession. She turned to her husband and said, 'He's not content with one poor go, not him!'

'What kind of a bull is he?' she asked the attendants. 'Oh, he's a working bull.'

Then they were shown a horse doing the same with a series of mares.

'What kind of horse is that?' the wife asked.

The farmhand replied, 'He's a workhorse.'

'Ah,' said the wife with a sigh, 'how fortunate are the wives of workmen!'

BARNYARD TRUTHS

The farmer's dignified elderly wife was bringing a group of city visitors around the farm.

Presently they came to the hen-house, and saw the hens contentedly pecking and preening. Suddenly a cock appeared, and with striding legs and flapping wings he made a bee-line for the nearest hen.

The visitors were wondering if the old lady was perhaps a little embarrassed that they should see what was certainly about to follow. But just then a poultry girl came into the yard, scattering food, and without a second's hesitation, the cock veered in his tracks and went for the grain.

The farmer's wife turned serenely to her guests and said, 'Isn't hunger a terrible thing?'

ZEBRA AND BULL

A zebra somehow managed to get loose from a zoo and wandered into the countryside.

He came to a farm where the first thing he saw was a sheep. 'What do you do?' asked the zebra.

'I grow wool.'

Then he saw a cow. 'What do you do?'

'I give milk.'

Next he saw a hen. 'What do you do?'

'I lay eggs.'

Then he saw a bull. 'What do you do?'

'Take off those pyjamas and I'll show you.'

RIDING ON THE BAR

After a late dance in the country, a boy brought a girl home on his bicycle.

She arrived red-faced and breathless. 'That was a wild ride,' she told her mother. 'Through the woods and all dark everywhere! I was sitting in front of Clarence, on the bar of his bike, and it sure was great.' She told everyone about it.

First chance he got, her father called her aside. 'If I were you,' he said, 'I wouldn't talk about that ride of yours. Everyone knows Clarence has a girl's bicycle, and it hasn't any bar.'

NEW VERSIONS

Mary had a little lamb –
  The midwife screamed.
But when Old MacDonald had a farm
  The doctor fainted.

STUCK IN THE MUD

They tell how in the old days a traveller was put up for the night along with the farmer and his wife in the only bed in the house. In the total darkness, while the farmer was asleep the other fellow got on top of the wife and went to town until the shaking of the bed began to wake the farmer.

Realising this, the traveller cried out as if dreaming, 'Gee-up, giddy-ap, gee-up, giddy-ap, giddy-ap now!'

The farmer, still half-asleep, mumbled, 'Listen, wife, the poor man thinks he's stuck in the mud and he's trying to rouse his horses.'

'But,' he added, 'he can't get out of that mud-hole unless he unloads.'

And he went back to sleep!

ALONG THE RIVER

There was an old woman who had a no-good husband. He never would do a day's work, just spent the hours in his boat on the river.

Once he hadn't turned up for some little time. The old woman was sitting by the fire one evening when two of the boys came rushing in, crying that the old man had been found – drowned.

The old lady didn't even look up and said nothing.

'And that isn't all,' added one of the boys. 'There were two big eels in his corpse!'

The old woman looked up when she heard that.

'Fetch me them eels,' she said, 'and set him again.'

GUARDING HER HONOUR

A rather simple country girl was invited to a wedding. Her mother was worried and warned her about the craftiness of men after they have been drinking. 'You must guard your honour,' she said. 'Be careful not to break it.'

At the wedding, the girl was so careful she held herself. A boy asked her why, and she explained.

'Oh,' he said, 'I'll fix it for you. I'll sew the opening together so that it can't fall out.'

He took her off to the barn and fixed her strongly. Then he stopped.

'No, no!' she cried. 'Don't stop. It needs more stitches.'

'I can't. I have no more thread.'

'Don't be silly. You have two balls of wool left.'

IN SCOTLAND

On a ferry crossing a loch, the boat sprang a leak, and the boatman seemed unable to locate the hole.

The passengers' feet were getting wetter and wetter all the time. 'Och,' said one of them, exasperated, 'if it had hair on it, ye'd find it!'

A NEW WORD FOR IT

The landowner's wife was looking over the harvest in a carriage driven by a young workman. She stood up to see better and fell head over heels to the ground, not hurting herself but revealing the embarrassing fact that she was wearing no underclothes – and the embarrassment itself.

To distract the youth, with great presence of mind she righted herself and jumped neatly back into the carriage. 'There!' she said to him, 'Did you see my agility?'

'Oh yes, ma'am,' he replied, blushing, 'I saw it!'

SHE KNEW WHAT SHE WANTED

A rich farmer's daughter had three suitors. Her parents said she would have to choose one of them.

So they were all invited to her father's house at the same time and were put up overnight in one big bed in the guest room. The girl hid in the attic above it to hear what they would say.

The first said, 'Listen to the wind and the rain! I hope they won't do harm to my cattle and the crops on my farms.'

The girl said to herself, 'He's rich. He's the man for me.'

Then the second said, 'A big storm is blowing up and the wind is from the west. I hope my fleet of ships will stay out of trouble.'

The girl said, 'He's even richer! He's the man for me.'

The third suitor kept silent, and the girl was about to go. Then he said, 'Move over, you two! Both of you are lying on my prick.'

The girl said, '*That*'s the man for me!'

118

EDUCATION

A country girl was sent away to university.

When she came home, her father met her at the station. She began to cry. 'Oh Pa,' she said, 'I ain't a virgin no more.'

The old man looked mighty glum. 'Me and your mother scrimped and saved all those years to send you to university. Now it looks like it was just money down the drain, because you still say *ain't*.'

IT WAS A GOOD ANSWER

A small farmer had to borrow to buy seed-corn, and he still hadn't sold the crop when the payment became due. This could be a disaster. What to do?

His wife, who was clever as well as pretty, said she would get the money from the factor by promising her favours in return. She would tell him her husband was away, but the husband would simply hide, and when she coughed twice he would appear.

All was done as planned. The money was given, the husband's debt was paid, the appointment was made, the husband hid, and as soon as she coughed twice he stormed in, and the factor ran away.

One of the city-folks hearing this story was disappointed. He said so to the farmer's wife.

'You should have coughed not before, but after the fun and games were over! Then all three of you would have been satisfied.'

She replied, 'Do you suppose we can all be as full of sense as your city ladies?'

THE VILLAGER AND HIS CALF

A village youth loses his calf and goes searching for it all through the village. But it's nowhere to be found, so eventually he climbs a tree to look over the countryside in the hope of seeing it.

A courting couple lie down beneath the tree and begin to make love. 'Kiss me, my treasure,' says the man to the girl. A little later he exclaims, 'Ye gods! what striking beauties I see.' And later still he cries out, 'Now I see the whole world!'

At this the youth calls down, 'Then tell me when you see my calf.'

ONE THING AT A TIME

A country girl said to her father, 'Dad, ain't you going to beat up that lorry-driver that throwed me down and ruin't me yesterday?'

The old man nodded vigorously. 'I sure am, daughter. But first I got to beat up that berry-picker that ruin't you last week.'

IN SCOTLAND

A husband and wife quarrelled because his apparatus was too short, with the result that he went to a wise-woman for a cure. She gave him an ointment.

He had only started on his way on the return journey, when it began to work. A girl coming towards him took one look and then accosted him! He was more than willing to oblige her, but just to get near enough to do it he had to cut off twelve inches.

When he reached home he put on more ointment, and soon after that was as high as a steeple. His happy wife was balanced on top while a crowd of watching women clamoured for their turn.

The wife called out to them

Farewell freens, farewell foes,
For I'm awa' to heaven
On a pintel's nose!

Sometimes a Granny comes into the act too. She is found pinned to the ceiling. 'Get an axe, get an axe!' They find one and prepare to cut her down, but she cries, 'No! Not that, you fools! Chop a hole in the ceiling and kiss Granny goodbye!'

THEY WANT THE MULE

An old woman moved in with her son-in-law who lived on a farm, and pretty soon a mule kicked the old lady to death. Everybody saw the big crowd that came to the house the next day, and someone remarked that the old lady certainly had a lot of friends.

The son-in-law said, 'Those fellows aren't here for the funeral. They're here to buy the mule.'

COMPROMISE

The dying wife's last request of her husband was that at her funeral he would ride in the same carriage with her mother.

'All right,' he finally said. 'But it will cast a gloom on the occasion.'

ANOTHER COMPROMISE

Another wife was dying. She said to her husband, 'I know you will marry again some day, and that's all right. She'll live in this house, too, and sleep in our bed and use my dishes, and that's all right. But I want you to promise me one thing, because I don't want your second wife to wear my clothes.'

The husband thought for a moment and then he said, 'All right, I promise. Your clothes wouldn't fit Betsy anyhow.'

THE RUNT

A farmer's dog came into town,
His Christian name was Runt.
A noble pedigree had he,
Noblesse oblige his stunt.

And as he trotted down the street,
'Twas beautiful to see
His work at every corner
And his work at every tree.

He watered every gateway too
And never missed a post,
For piddling was his specialty,
And piddling was his boast.

The city curs looked on amazed
With deep and jealous rage,
To see a simple country dog
The piddler of the age.

Then all the dogs from everywhere
Were summoned by a yell
To sniff the country stranger o'er
And judge him by his smell.

Some thought that he a king might be,
Beneath his tail a rose.
So every city dog drew nigh
And sniffed it up his nose.

They smelled him over one by one,
They smelled him two by two,
And noble Runt, in high disdain,
Stood still 'til they were through.

Then just to show the whole shebang
He didn't give a damn,
He trotted to a grocery store
And piddled on a ham.

He piddled in a mackerel keg,
He piddled on the floor,
And when the grocer kicked him out
He piddled through the door.

Behind him all the city dogs
Lined up with instinct true,
To start a piddling carnival
And see the stranger through.

They showed him every piddling post
They had in all the town,
And started in, with many a wink,
To pee the stranger down.

They sent for champion piddlers who
Were always on the go,
Who sometimes did a piddling stunt
Or gave a piddling show.

They sprung these on him suddenly
When midway in the town,
Runt only smiled and polished off
The ablest, white and brown.

For Runt was with them every trick,
With vigour and with vim.
A thousand piddlers more or less
Were all the same to him.

So he was wetting merrily
With hind leg kicking high,
When most were hoisting legs in bluff
And piddling mighty dry.

Then on and on Runt sought new grounds,
By piles of scrap and rust,
Till every city dog went dry
And only piddled dust.

But ever on went noble Runt
As wet as any rill,
And all the champion city pups
Were peed to a standstill.

Then Runt did freehand piddling,
With fancy flirts and flings,
Like double drip and gimlet twist,
And all that sort of thing.

And all the time this country dog
Did never wink nor grin,
But piddled blithely out of town
As he came piddling in.

Envoi:
The city dogs, convention held
To ask, 'What did defeat us?'
But no one ever put them wise
That Runt had diabetes.

SALLY

I don't know what's become of Sally –
It was no fault of mine.
I wonder what's become of Sally –
I put her in the hay,
And then I went away.
Of course, I must admit,
I rode her quite a bit,
But from what I know now,
Someone else was doing it.
I wonder what's become of Sally,
That old mare of mine.

In the City

IN A LONDON CLUB

A retired Brigadier and his Guards son were having a drink together in their London club. An American was sitting very near them.

The Brigadier was deaf and left it to his son to conduct conversations. Seeing the American he said, 'Ask that fellow if this is his first visit to England.'

The son did. 'No,' he bawled to his father, 'The Colonel says he was over here during the war.'

'Ask him where he was stationed.'

This was duly relayed. 'In Suffolk.'

'What part of Suffolk?'

'Near Brandon.'

'Extraordinary! Ask where.'

'Near Icknield Grange.'

'Really! Ask him if he knew Lady Amelia.'

With that question, the American grew very animated. 'Did I know her? I'll say I did! What a baby! And did she throw parties! That dame was a real hot number.'

'What did the fellow say?' asked the Brigadier.

'Says he knew Mother, Father.'

THE LONG OF IT

One night two black men were walking along the upper level of the bridge at Newcastle-on-Tyne when they were taken short. They relieved themselves over the railing.

'My, this river's cold!' said the first one.

'And deep,' said the second.

CRISPS

A big fat woman was standing one evening on a street in Glasgow, attracting shocked notice from passers-by. She was eating potato-crisps which she had poured into her apron. Lifting the apron, she had also lifted her skirts, and was in fact starkers from the waist down.

Someone called a policeman. He said, 'What do you think you're doing, Annie? You with your skirts in the air, making a display of yourself!'

'Oh,' she said, looking down. 'Is the wee sailor gone?'

MINE!

A man was given a double room in a hotel and had just unpacked, when the manager came up and asked if he would take a single room and allow a honeymoon couple to have this one. The man agreed.

After he had moved to the new room and again unpacked, he realised that he'd left his umbrella behind. He went back to get it but paused outside the door. He could hear what the couple were saying.

The husband: To whom do those beautiful blonde curls belong?

Wife: To you, darling, they're all yours.

Husband: And your lovely blue eyes?

Wife: They're yours, darling, yours!

Husband: And those kissable lips?

Wife: Yours, darling.

Husband: And that white throat?

Wife: Yours, yours!

And so on, until the man outside could stand it no longer. He called through the door, 'When you come to the umbrella, that's mine!'

FAIR IS FAIR

Two men started chatting in a bar and then had a couple of drinks together.

'Look,' said one, 'I want to treat you now, but I've no more money with me. I'll just go back to my flat and get some from my wife. Why don't you come along?'

'Sure,' said the other.

The man's flat was just a few steps away, and they went up to the first floor. Inside it in full view, doors wide open, the man's wife was in bed with another man. The acquaintance from the bar was shocked and embarrassed, but the husband kept his cool.

'Got some money?' he asked his wife.

'Sure. Look in my purse. It's over there on the dresser.'

The husband did, found some, and motioning to his new friend, led the way out and back to the pub.

'Two more of the same,' he said to the barkeeper.

The second man was too amazed by what he'd seen to say a word. Finally he asked, 'But what about the man in the bed?'

'Oh, he can buy his own drink,' said the husband.

ALL THE SAME

In Sheffield she was Sheila,
*   Down in London she was Lu.*
In Reddish she was Ruby
*   With lips like morning dew.*
In Manchester she was Mary,
*   The finest of the bunch,*
But down in his expenses
*   She was petrol, oil and lunch.*

THE BIGGEST

During the war, three mothers met on a London street, and it turned out that each of them had a daughter in the armed forces.

The first one said, 'My daughter is doing very well indeed. She's been in the WAVES. for only six months, and she's already saved five hundred pounds.'

The second one laughed. 'That's nothing! My daughter is in the WACS, and in a year she's saved twelve-hundred pounds.'

The third spoke up. 'My daughter is in the TUTES. She's been in only for three months, and she's already saved two thousand pounds!'

The others said, 'The TUTES, the TUTES? What branch of the service is that?'

'Oh, the biggest branch. The Prostitutes.'

SILENCED

In a posh suburb an executive put on some old clothes and went out to cut the lawn. A woman came along in a Rolls-Royce and noticed what a good job he was doing.

She hailed him and said, 'How much do they pay you for this kind of work?'

'I don't get any money,' he said.

'You don't get any money?'

'No. Instead, the lady that lives here, she lets me sleep with her.'

The woman drove off, fast.

THE OFFICE PARTY

Dear Friends,

When I came into the office this morning, I noticed a sort of general feeling of unfriendliness, and since several of you have openly called me a dirty son-of-a-bitch to my face, I know I must have done something wrong at our office party last Friday. As this is my last day, I'd like to take this way of apologising to all of you. I would rather speak to everyone personally, but you all seem to go deaf and dumb whenever I try to talk with you.

First, to our dear and beloved boss, Mr Simons, I am sorry for all the things I called you on Friday afternoon. I am very much aware that your father is not a baboon, nor is your mother a whore. Your wife is a delightful woman, and my story of buying her for 50p. in Tiajuana was strictly a figment of my imagination. Your children are undoubtedly yours too. About the water cooler incident, well . . . you'll never know how badly I feel about it, and I hope they didn't hurt your head when they were trying to get the glass jug off.

To comely Miss Ashby, I express my deepest regrets. In my own defence I must remind you that you seemed to enjoy our little escapade on the stairway as much as I did, until the banister broke and we fell eight feet to the second floor landing. In spite of the rupture you incurred when I landed on top of you, I'm sure you will admit that when we landed, it was one of the biggest thrills you've ever had.

Sam Franklin, you old cuss, you've got to forgive me for the little prank I played on you. If I had known you were goosy, I'd never have done it. It could have been a lot worse if that fat lady hadn't been standing right under the window you jumped through; she broke your fall a lot. People have been killed falling through windows.

Mr Gray, I regret telling the fireman that it was you

who turned in the false alarm, but of course I had no way of knowing they would be such bad sports about it. Those fire hoses sure have a lot of pressure, don't they? And the water is so cold!

Bill Granfield, you rate a special apology. My laughing when you forgot to put the seat down and got stuck in the John was bad enough, but my calling everyone else into the rest room was unforgivable.

Bill Thompson, I know how you must feel about me . . . opening the door to the mop closet suddenly must have startled you and Miss Finch quite badly, and when I think of how hard you bumped your chin on the sink when you bent over to pull up your pants, it makes me sick! We'll have to get together for dinner some night after the dentist finishes your plates.

Miss Brown, the only excuse I can offer for stealing your clothes and hiding them when you passed out in the ladies' room, is that I was drunk. Also, I want you to know I was so embarrassed when I couldn't remember where I hid them, and you had to go home in that old sofa cover. Running your falsies out on the flagpole was a bit too much, I guess, but like I said – I was drunk.

To all the rest of you, I am sorry . . . setting Mrs Botts' lace panties on fire seemed like a funny idea at the time, and it makes me sad to hear that her husband is getting a divorce because of what I did.

Now that I have apologised to all of you and know I will be forgiven, I've got a big surprise for you. Even though I don't work here any more, I am going to do my best to get back for the office picnic next Friday.

Your friend and ex co-worker.

CHARADE

Charades were a favourite pastime in one set. They grew more and more inspired and more and more inventive.

One night the host divided the company into teams, all the men on one side and all the women on the other. In due course it was the men's turn to guess what the women were portraying. There was a lot of giggling and squealing behind the scenes as the ladies got ready.

When the lights went on, the men gasped. The women were in a single line, stark naked, but some of them were facing front and some were facing the rear.

Several husbands were angry; others were abashed. The bachelors whistled and cheered and could hardly stay in their seats. But no one could guess the answer.

'We give up, we give up!' they yelled. 'What is it?'

'A military band,' said the host.

They were as puzzled as ever. 'How come?'

'Titty-bum, titty-bum, titty-bum bum bum,' he explained.

HE ASKED

The rich boyfriend of a showgirl asked her, 'Would you still love me if I lost my money?'

'Of course, darling,' she said. 'I'd miss you too.'

AFTER HOURS

One night a bobby is walking down a street where there are three parked cars. He shines his torch in the window of the first car and says, 'Hello hello hello, and what do you think you're doing?'

'We're doing the waltz.'

The same thing happens with the next car. 'Hello hello hello, and what do you think you're doing?'

'We're doing the fox-trot.'

At the third car he says, 'I suppose you're doing the Bossa Nova?'

Girl's voice: 'No, officer, I'm doing the boss a favour.'

MATURITY

In a big city, a foursome of middle-aged ladies met once a week to play bridge. They were very upset when one of them moved away and they had to find a new fourth.

After much deliberation, they invited Mrs Edwards, who was perhaps a cut below them socially. But they agreed that she would have to keep to their standards of behaviour.

So hardly had Mrs Edwards arrived and seated herself, when one of them said in an austere tone, 'You must observe the conventional rules at this table. There are some subjects we never discuss. We never discuss husbands. They are all impossible. We never discuss coats or motorcars. We all have furs and limousines. We never discuss grandchildren. All our grandchildren are geniuses. And we never discuss sex. What was, was!'

ETIQUETTE

Two old street-walkers were fighting over a customer one night on a dimly-lit street in Dublin.

One of them finally prevailed. She hooked her arm in the man's, and led him off to Saint Patrick's Cathedral, no less, behind the steps there. But they couldn't shake the other one; she followed them as far as the front of the steps.

When the couple reappeared, the man paid the woman. Up comes the other old girl with her hand out.

'Penny for the bridesmaid, sir?'

THE TWELVE DAYS OF CHRISTMAS

> Miss Agnes McHolstein
> 69 Cash Avenue
> Beaver Valley, Colorado
> December 14, 1982

Dearest John,
  I went to the door today and the postman delivered a partridge in a pear tree. What a thoroughly delightful gift. I couldn't have been more surprised.
> With deepest love and devotion,
>   Agnes

> Miss Agnes McHolstein
> 69 Cash Avenue
> Beaver Valley, Colorado
> December 15, 1982

Dearest John,
  Today the postman brought your very sweet gift. Just imagine two turtle doves. I'm just delighted at your very thoughtful gift. They are just adorable.
> All my love,
>   Agnes

Miss Agnes McHolstein
69 Cash Avenue
Beaver Valley, Colorado
December 16, 1982

Dear John,
   Oh! Aren't you the extravagant one. Now I really must protest. I don't deserve such generosity, three French hens. They are just darling but I must insist, you've been too kind.
                    Love,

                                   Agnes

Miss Agnes McHolstein
69 Cash Avenue
Beaver Valley, Colorado
December 17, 1982

Dear John,
   Today the postman delivered 4 calling birds. Now really, they are beautiful but don't you think enough is enough. You're being too romantic.
                    Affectionately,

                                   Agnes

Miss Agnes McHolstein
69 Cash Avenue
Beaver Valley, Colorado
December 18, 1982

Dearest John,

What a surprise. Today the postman delivered 5 golden rings; one for every finger. You're just impossible, but I love it. Frankly, all those birds squawking were beginning to get on my nerves.

All my love,

Agnes

Miss Agnes McHolstein
69 Cash Avenue
Beaver Valley, Colorado
December 19, 1982

Dear John,

When I opened the door there were actually 6 geese a-laying on my front steps. So you're back to the birds again – huh? Those geese are huge. Where will I ever keep them? The neighbours are complaining and I can't sleep through the racket.

Please stop.

Cordially,

Agnes

Miss Agnes McHolstein
69 Cash Avenue
Beaver Valley, Colorado
December 20, 1982

John,

What's with you and those fucking birds?? 7 swans a-swimming. What kind of God damn joke is this? There's bird shit all over the house and they never stop with the racket. I can't sleep at night and I'm a nervous wreck, it's not funny. So stop with those fucking birds.

Sincerely,

Agnes

Miss Agnes McHolstein
69 Cash Avenue
Beaver Valley, Colorado
December 21, 1982

OK Buster,

I think I prefer the birds. What the hell am I going to do with 8 maids a-milking? It's not enough with all those birds and 8 maids a-milking, but they had to bring their God damn cows. There is shit all over the lawn and I can't move in my own house. Just lay off me, smartass.

Agnes

Miss Agnes McHolstein
69 Cash Avenue
Beaver Valley, Colorado
December 22, 1982

Hey shithead,
  What are you? Some kind of sadist. Now there's 9
pipers playing. And Christ do they play. They've never
stopped chasing those maids since they got here
yesterday morning. The cows are getting upset and
they're stepping all over those screeching birds. What
am I going to do? The neighbours have started a
petition to evict me.
                    You'll get yours,

                                    Agnes

Miss Agnes McHolstein
69 Cash Avenue
Beaver Valley, Colorado
December 23, 1982

You rotten prick,
  Now there's 10 ladies dancing. I don't know why I call
those sluts ladies. They've been balling those pipers all
night long. Now the cows can't sleep and they've got the
diarrhoea. My living room is a river of shit. The
Commissioner of Buildings has subpoenaed me to give
cause why the building shouldn't be condemned.
  I'm sticking the police on you.
                        One who means it

Miss Agnes McHolstein
69 Cash Avenue
Beaver Valley, Colorado
December 24, 1982

Listen fuckhead,
    What's with the 11 lords a-leaping on those maids and
ladies? Some of those broads will never walk again.
Those pipers ran through the maids and have been
committing sodomy with the cows. All 23 of the birds
are dead. They've been trampled to death in the orgy. I
hope you're satisfied you rotten vicious swine.

                                          Your sworn enemy

Law Offices
Badger, Bedner and
Cahole
303 Knave Street
Chicago, Illinois
December 25, 1982

Dear Sir:
    This is to acknowledge your latest gift of 12 fiddlers
fiddling which you have seen fit to inflict on our client,
Miss Agnes McHolstein. The destruction of course was
total. All correspondence should come to our attention.
If you should attempt to reach Miss McHolstein at
Happy Dale Sanitarium, the attendants have instruc-
tions to shoot you on sight. With this letter please find
attached a warrant for your arrest.
                    Cordially,
                        Badger, Bedner and Cahole

PICCADILLY

I'm sure you can imagine
It's easy as can be,
The place is Piccadilly,
The people – he and she.

She whispered, 'Will it hurt me?'
'Of course not,' said he,
'It's a very simple process.
Just let me move this knee.'

She said, 'I'm rather frightened,
I've not had this before.'
So he started to convince her
It would not hurt at all.

She finally consented,
Tears were in her eyes.
'It's hurting rather badly!
It must be quite a size.'

'Now calm yourself, my darling,'
His face portrayed a grin.
'Just open a little wider
So I can get it in.'

'It's coming now,' he told her.
'I know,' she said. 'It's wet.'
She felt him pushing upward,
He said, 'Keep still, my pet.'

Suddenly it soaked her.
She gave a startled shout.
'It's coming now,' he muttered,
'Thank God we got it out!'

Now if you've read this carefully
And given yourself a thrill,
You'll find that he's a dentist
With other teeth to fill.

STRIP POKER

Betty and Billy, myself and fair Milly,
  Once sat in a strip-poker game.
All of us truly were young and unruly
  But the pep it was there just the same.

The cards that I had were running quite bad,
  Then suddenly they came to me great!
From out of the slush, I cornered a flush
  Of diamonds, the four to the eight.

Betty and Billy dropped out, leaving Milly
  And yours truly to fight it alone.
I raised it a tie and, flick of me eye,
  She saw it and raised it a comb.

This kinda hurt, I saw with my shirt,
  With a coat I raised in great haste.
She looked with her belt, and saying, 'You dealt,' '
  She boosted it high with her waist.

But I didn't flinch, it looked like a cinch,
  So I bet every stitch that I had.
She saw, if you please, with her silken chemise
  And — (stopped by the censors) — too bad!

French and Others

CLEAR SPEECH

At a big diplomatic party in London, an Englishman was struggling to make conversation with a Frenchman who was struggling to speak correct English.

'Do you come to London often?' the Englishman asked.

'Ah, yes, monsieur.'

'You like it?'

'Ah, but of course, monsieur. It is just that I miss a little my familee.'

'You have left your family in Paris, monsieur?'

'Oh yes, my wife.'

'And children perhaps?'

'No, monsieur.'

'Oh, they come along soon enough.'

'Non, non, not in my case, hélas! The difficulty is with my wife, monsieur. My wife, she is – how you say it – my wife she is – inconceivable. No, no! That is the wrong word. That is not what I mean!'

'Ah?'

'My wife, my wife she is – she is – unbearable! No, no – that is not what I mean.'

A pause.

Then, 'My wife, my wife she is – intangible! No, no – that is not what I mean.'

Then, victory!

'My wife, my wife, she is – inscrutable!'

ANCIENT ROAMIN'

In ancient Rome, the Emperor Augustus was startled to find a poor man from the provinces who looked exactly like him.

He laughed and royally joked, 'I suppose your mother used to come to Rome.'

'No,' said the countryman, 'but my father did.'

NOT AT FAULT

In Italy a wife came weeping to her father. She said her husband was going to repudiate her because she was barren.

'And it isn't my fault!' she cried.

Putting it as delicately as he could, her father said that she should, if necessary, try someone other than her husband.

'Oh,' she sobbed, 'I have tried! I tried all the manservants, even the stableboys!'

Her father consoled her. He told her she was utterly blameless for being without children.

THE STATUE ADJUSTED

When a statue in a French bachelor's house was damaged, he ordered from the manufacturer replacement pieces for the missing parts.

These were delivered, and the maid glued them on. Thus it happened that the penis on the statue, which originally had been hanging down, was now facing up.

When the master scolded the maid for this, she said, 'It's just like you when Mademoiselle Yvette goes to your bed! I've never seen any of them otherwise.'

MATURE AND PREMATURE

In Spain, two elderly maiden ladies were having tea at their sister's house when her young son arrived home from school.

'What happened in school today, dear?' they asked.

'Teacher said an American ship was coming, filled up with sailors who haven't touched land for months, and they are mad like bulls! He said they are going to rape all the women in sight!'

Shocked, the two maiden aunts got up and left the house.

'What's the hurry?' asked the boy. 'The ship isn't arriving until the day after tomorrow.'

THE CUSTOMER IS HARD TO TALK TO IN THIS POSITION

Scene: a brothel in Belgium. The English regular is to be satisfied. He isn't.

He complains to the Madam and then marches out, shoulders back, moustaches flying.

The girl is called up for questioning. She is very indignant. She explains to the Madam. 'He put his cock in my mouth, then his two balls, and then he said, 'Now cry "Vive le Hangleterre!" I couldn't do all that at once!'

THE GOVERNMENT STALLION

Some time ago in Picardy, it was decreed that those married couples who in two years did not produce a child would be visited by an official child-begetter.

One such officer duly called on a childless man and wife. He told them the rates for his services depended on the depth of entry. For five francs they would get a peasant, for ten a curé, for fifteen a notary, twenty a lawyer, twenty-five a bishop or a high functionary.

'Choose, my good man,' he said.

The husband decided that a peasant would do, and the official got to work.

The wife wanted him in deeper, so the husband hit him on his backside.

'See, wife,' he said, 'it wasn't necessary to give him twenty francs more!'

ETHNIC AGAIN

The French were guillotining foreigners. Each prisoner could choose whether to lie under it face up or face down.

The first was an Englishman. He chose face up. The blade got caught just short of his throat, and he was allowed to go free.

The next was a Scotsman. He also chose face up, and the same thing happened to him. He too was allowed to go free.

The next was an Irishman. He also chose face up. Then he said, 'Just a minute. I think I see what your trouble is.'

THE TWO MOUTHS

In Ostend there was a big fair, and three country girls went to see it.

After they had spent all their money in the shops, they came across the big exhibition tent. They very much wanted to go in, but their pockets were empty. They explained this to the man in charge, who said they could go in free if they could answer his question correctly: Which of their two mouths was the oldest?

The first girl said, 'The top mouth is the oldest because it has teeth.'

The second said, 'The bottom is, because it has a beard.'

The third said, 'The oldest is the top mouth because the bottom mouth still needs to be fed. It was fed this very morning by our servant.'

The man decided that this was the best answer.

He said to that girl, 'It merits a special recompense, and I have the means to give it to you. Come and see me later.'

PATRIOTISM

A French father was uneasy when a stranger became interested in his daughter. Then it happened that for some reason the young man was going to call at their home late one evening, and the father became more nervous. He was tired and wanted to go to his own room and go to sleep, but he didn't want to leave the young people alone.

He took his daughter aside and said, 'I hope that young man is indeed a gentleman and that he knows what is proper.'

'Oh yes, papa, I'm sure he will do as he should.'

'Very well, my daughter. But if he gives you any trouble, you must just call out, "Papa, papa!" and I will come right down.'

'Yes, papa. Thank you, papa. But what if we're only having a laugh, good fun, you know?'

'Ah yes. What then? Oh – then in that case just sing the Marseillaise.'

'Yes, papa.'

Late in the night the father was awakened by a sound. 'Papa, papa, papa!' He sprang up to investigate, but then the sound became PaPA, paPA, paPA, PA PA PA PA pa PA – to the tune of the Marseillaise.

FROM DIDEROT

The great French writer Diderot tells of a call-house in Paris where a little man was discovered to have 'the most imposing figure'.

But, says Diderot, one of the girls turned him around and remarked, 'That's all very well, but tell me, where is the backside that will drive it?'

TIN LIZZIE

A peasant sorcerer in Italy had great local fame as a caster of spells. One of his neighbours repeatedly asked him if he would turn his (the neighbour's) wife into an automobile! He explained that he needed a car much more than he needed a wife.

The wife was more than a little simple and very pretty; the husband was even simpler and very insistent. So the sorcerer was finally prevailed on to cast the spell. It was arranged that he would come to the couple's house on a certain evening.

When he arrived, he explained that silence was essential during the transformation. They would all three proceed to the barn where there would be room for the automobile. He would utter the right incantations and then go through the right rituals, and the enchantment would then take place. The first ritual would be for the wife to remove all her clothing; then he, the magician, would remove his. The husband would hold on high a big torch to provide light. But, he said, remember, silence on the part of the couple was absolutely necessary.

All went as planned. They went to the barn. The wife stripped, and then as directed by the sorcerer, she got down on all fours. The sorcerer then stripped and stood behind her and chanted strange words, edging nearer to her all the time. Part of him was getting very near indeed!

The husband was growing uneasy. 'Er –' he began.

'Silence!' thundered the magician. Then he reminded him, 'Keep quiet, and you'll soon see how the engine works. Just wait until I get the crank in!'

'I don't want the kind of car that needs a crank!' shouted the husband, shaking the heavy torch.

'Now you've done it. You've ruined the spell!' cried the sorcerer, as he grabbed his clothes and ran away.

GREEKS

A Greek farmer trapped his wife with three of his workmen. One was under the bed, one behind the curtains, and the third in the wardrobe.

He lined them up and told them if they didn't want trouble, they must do as he said. Each was to go to the fields and return with a vegetable.

The first workman returned with a beet. The farmer shoved it up his backside while he screamed.

The second brought back a cucumber. The same thing happened – the farmer shoved that up his backside while he screamed. But suddenly he stopped screaming and started to laugh.

'What's so funny?' demanded the farmer.

'Look. Here comes Vassili with a watermelon!'

THE MORNING AFTER

Italian girl: Now you will hate me.

Spanish girl: For this I shall love you always.

Russian girl: My body has belonged to you, but my soul will always remain free.

American girl: Who are you? I must have been drunk.

German girl: After we rest a while, maybe we go to a beer garden, yah?

Swedish girl: I tank I go home now.

French girl: For this I get a new dress, wee?

Jewish girl: I should have held out for a fur coat.

Coloured girl: Boss, ah sho hope this done change yo luck.

Chinese girl: Now you know it isn't so.

English girl: There, dear, do you feel better now?

GOTCHA!

A girl was nervous of travelling in the Balkans because of her fear of the vampires for which the locality was notorious. Whenever she went to sleep, she was careful to keep her crucifix within reach.

She stopped overnight at an inn in a Jewish area and went to bed. She awoke at midnight and in absolute terror saw a vampire approaching. Quickly she seized the crucifix and held it between herself and him.

'Dot vun't protect you, darlink!' he said.

THE BET

John Fourteen-Times bets a widow two of his best cows against two of hers that he will do his usual fourteen times in one night.

She marks the wall each time, but the total is only twelve. He says she forgot two.

'No, no.'

'But yes!' he claims.

'Let's not argue,' she says, and wipes out the score. He is very relieved.

Then she snuggles up and adds, 'Instead, let's begin again.'

THE SPANISH NOBILIO

There once was a Spanish Nobilio,
Who lived in an ancient castillio.
He was proud of his tra la la lillio
And the works of his tweedle dum dee!

One day he went to the theatillio.
And there saw a lovely dancillio
Who excited his tra la la lillio,
And the works of his tweedle dum dee!

He took her up to his castillio,
And laid her upon his sofillio,
Then inserted his tra la la lillio,
And the works of his tweedle dum dee!

Nine days later he saw the doctillio –
He had a fine dose of clapillio
All over his tra la la lillio,
And the works of his tweedle dum dee!

Now he sits in his castillio,
With a handful of cotton-wadillio;
He swabs off his tra la la lillio
And the works of his tweedle dum dee!

HINKY DINKY PARLEZ-VOUS

Mademoiselle from Armenteers, parlez-vous,
Mademoiselle from Armenteers, parlez-vous.
Mademoiselle from Armenteers,
Hasn't been kissed in forty years.
Hinky dinky parlez-vous.

Mademoiselle from Armenteers, parlez-vous,
Mademoiselle from Armenteers, parlez-vous.
She went to church and said her prayers,
While her daughter ran the joint upstairs.
Hinky dinky parlez-vous.

– She wore her dresses awful loose,
And waggled her headlights and caboose.

– She's the hardest-working girl in town,
And she makes her living laying down.

Mademoiselle from gay Paree, parlez-vous,
Mademoiselle from gay Paree, parlez-vous.
Oh, the Corporal went to gay Paree,
And now it hurts like hell to – gee!
Hinky dinky parlez-vous.

– She gave a wink, and said, 'Oui, oui!'
'Oh, fireman, turn the hose on me!'

– The only thing that she gave free,
The doctors took away from me.

Mademoiselle from Chateauroo, parlez-vous,
Mademoiselle from Chateauroo, parlez-vous.
Mademoiselle from Chateauroo,
Enough for her is too much for you.
Hinky dinky parlez-vous.

SHRINKAGE

A Frenchman made a habit of sleeping with whatever maid it was that cleaned his flat. None of them stayed very long, and it happened that this night it was the turn of a new one.

He was somewhat puzzled. He asked her later if she was a virgin – he had found the fit very narrow, he said.

'Oh', she said, 'did not monsieur see that he put his shirt in along with himself?'

In the East

WELL ENOUGH

An Arab king was returning home after a long trip.
When he and his company were nearing his city, they
happened to meet on the road one of the royal servants.

'How have things fared in our absence?' the king
asked him.

'Well enough, Oh noble lord.'

'Was there any mishap at all?'

'Alas, noble sir, our best dog died.'

'How did it die?'

'A mule got frightened and tried to break loose, and
as it lunged forward it trampled on the dog.'

'What frightened the mule?'

'He was tied up in the stable when the stable caught
fire.'

'What happened to him?'

'He was burned up along with the stable.'

'How did the stable come to burn?'

'It caught on fire when the palace burned.'

'You mean my palace is burned down?' the king
exclaimed.

'Alas, yes, Oh noble lord.'

'How did it catch fire?'

'From one of the gold-fringed rugs hanging on the
walls.'

'How did the rug catch fire?'

'From a candle.'

'But why was a candle put near the hangings?'

'The candles were lit on your mother-in-law's coffin.'

'You mean that my mother-in-law is dead?' the king
asked without too much distress.

'Yes, noble lord.'

'What was the matter with her?'

156

'Well, it was like this. Your wife the queen ran off with your vizier, and her mother got so nervous and worked up she just died.'

PAVILIONS

One Friday night a Muslim wife came home from the Mosque and told her husband about the sermon.

'The preacher said that if you fulfil your matrimonial duties, you get a pavilion in Paradise. Just think, God wants houses there for us all!'

'Come on, then,' said the husband. 'Let's build a pavilion in Paradise.'

Afterward, the husband wanted to sleep. But the wife said, 'You only built yourself a house, now build me one!'

'No,' said the husband. 'You must not get big ideas. One house will have to do for both of us.'

HIDING-PLACE

A young Turkish wife was at the baths one afternoon when a robbery took place there. Her husband heard the news of this, and as soon as he returned home that evening he asked her what had happened.

'Did they get those valuable rings I gave you?'

'Oh no,' she said, blushing. 'You know I always keep those with me at the baths.'

'But the thieves took many jewels, they say.'

'They did. But I had hidden mine in the usual – er – hole.'

'Oh, of course, of course! Very good! But what about your handbag with all your money, and your new wrap, and those shoes from Paris?'

She said indignantly, 'You know perfectly well there isn't room enough for all of that!'

'Ah, so. But what a pity that you didn't have your mother with you.'

THE FIFTH VEDA

In the East, a wife wanted to get rid of her husband so that she would have more time with her lover. So she told him that the authorities were jailing all the men who didn't know the Fifth Veda, and that he should leave immediately and not return until he'd learned it. The husband obediently set forth.

Outside his village he met five ladies and told them his story. 'Aha!' said the first lady. 'All of us know the Fifth Veda. Come with me, and I'll teach you the first part.'

She brought him to her home. Her husband was away. Her servants prepared a delicious dinner for them, but in the midst of it, she suddenly screamed. The men of the household rushed in. 'Oh, it's all right,' she told them. 'My nephew here choked, and I thought he would die! But as you see, he is fine now.'

They went away. 'You know now what would happen if I screamed again?' she said. And so she made him do what she wanted.

On the next morning she told him that he had now learned the first part of the Fifth Veda, and she sent him to the second lady.

The second lady was a farmer's wife. She led the young man to her husband. 'Husband,' she said, 'I bet the shopkeeper's wife that you could milk a cow blindfolded without spilling a drop. This young man is to be witness.'

While the husband was milking, she beckoned to the man, who quickly learned the second section.

The third lady put him into a lodging-house, then went home and pretended to be very ill. She asked her husband to send to the lodging for a woman friend of hers who knew about this sickness. Dressed as a woman, the young man came to the sickroom and in due form prescribed for her complaint.

The fourth lady hid him in her orchard. She told her

husband a tree there was enchanted. Whoever climbed the tree saw magical things. The husband climbed it and soon saw his wife and the young man intimately engaged. While he angrily descended, the young man went on his way, and the husband found his wife quite alone. She then climbed the tree and claimed to see her husband in the same activity.

The fifth lady pretended to be insane. The young man posed as a famous physician. He said she was possessed by an evil spirit. He directed the servants to clean the house, scent it, and strew flowers about. Then he had the wife put into a closed litter which he also entered, and while four men carried it four times around the house, to music, he learned the last section of the Fifth Veda.

NO CHOICE

An old woman was asked if she would rather have Turkish Delight, chocolates, or a man.

'My child, you know I don't have teeth to eat sweets.'

MOTHER-IN-LAW AGAIN

At the party before the wedding in Cyprus, the bride's mother was told that the groom lacked the necessary equipment. All the bride's family was aghast. Could it be true? The bride was in tears. What to do?

The bride's mother announced that she would see for herself and report back. She would go to where the groom was dressing for the wedding and would hold an inspection.

Off she went.

His equipment was in fact not only there, but so active that it knocked off her spectacles, which landed on top of it.

Beaming, she hurried back and said to the assembled crowd, 'Everything is OK. I saw something and it was wearing glasses.'

HUSBANDS AGAIN

A wife was not satisfied with the irregular attentions of her husband, and finally got him to agree that they would have sexual relations on Fridays.

'Every Friday?' asked the husband.

'Every Friday.'

'But how will I remember?' he asked.

'I'll put your turban on the chest.'

One day, it was not Friday but the wife was very much in the mood. So she put the turban on the chest.

The husband was surprised. 'But it's not Friday!' he said.

'Yes it is.'

'Well, something's wrong. It doesn't matter whether it's Friday or me, but one will have to wait on the other.'

THE THREE WISHES

On the Night of Power, a man said to his wife, 'Hark! God hath proclaimed to me from the invisible world that three wishes will be granted unto me, so do thou counsel me what shall I ask.'

She said, 'The perfection of man and his delight is his yard, so do thou pray God to greaten thy yard and magnify it.'

Hardly had he spoken this prayer when his yard became as big as a calabash and he could neither sit nor stand nor move; and when he would have lain with his wife, she fled before him from place to place.

So he said to her, 'Oh accursed woman, what is to be done? This is thy wish, by reason of thy lust!'

'By Allah!' she answered, 'I did not ask for this huge bulk, for which the gate of a street were too narrow. Pray God to make it less.'

So he raised his eyes to heaven and said, 'Oh my God, rid me of this thing and deliver me therefrom.'

And immediately his yard disappeared altogether, and he became smooth as a woman.

When his wife saw this, she cried, 'I have no occasion for thee, now thou art become yardless!'

He replied, 'I had three prayers accepted of God, wherewith I might have gotten my good, both in this world and the next, and now two are gone in pure waste, by thy lewd wish.'

'By Allah!' she exclaimed. 'I did not ask for this!'

'Still,' he continued, 'with the one that remains, what do you say? Should we wish for Paradise in the next life, or for healthy old age, or for vast riches?'

'No.' And she directed him, 'Instead pray God the most high to restore thee thy yard as it was.'

God did.

LOVER'S GIFT REGAINED

An Eastern ruler was about to execute his favourite wife because she had had an affair. He was very annoyed. His chief minister, however, advised him to forgive her, inasmuch as this was an unimportant triviality.

'She is simply a woman,' he said. 'All women are the same. Come, your Highness, I will show you their deceitfulness and wickedness. Let us disguise ourselves and make a journey together to see what we see.'

Soon after they had started out, they saw coming towards them a wedding procession. The groom's father came first, then the young bride in a closed carriage ornamented with velvet and gold. Behind it walked brightly-dressed women and slaves, and behind them came a large escort of horsemen.

The chief minister said, 'If you like, your Highness, you can make this bride misconduct herself with you.'

'What are you saying! With this great escort of hers it would be impossible.'

'I will show you.'

The minister put up a tent and had the ruler go inside. Then he himself sat by the side of the road, weeping.

The father of the groom, at the head of the procession, came up to them. He asked the minister what was wrong.

'My wife is about to have a child, and I set out to bring her to her own people. But the pangs overtook her on the way. I don't know what do do! I cannot go to her, and alas! there is no woman with us.'

'That's easily remedied,' said the groom's father. 'There are many women in this procession. One of them can attend her.'

'In that case, please let this maiden go. It will bring her good luck.'

'So it will,' thought the groom's father. 'It will augur fertility.'

So the girl went into the tent, fell in love at first sight with the ruler, and soon did what he wished. He gave her his ring, and she left. The procession moved on.

The chief minister came up to the ruler and said, 'You see? Even this girl, young as she is, is willing to deceive. How much more is this true of married women! Did you give her anything, your Highness?'

'Yes, my ring.'

'I shall not let her keep it!'

The minister followed in haste and caught up with the carriage. He told them, 'This girl has gone off with a ring which my lady wife had laid on the pillow. Give it back, lady!'

Handing him the ring, she scratched his hand. 'Take it, you rogue!' she said.

THE FIVE GALLANTS

In her husband's prolonged absence, a lady fell in love with a handsome young man, and he with her. One day the youth was sent to prison on some trivial complaint made about him to the chief of police. The lady was nearly frantic. However, she put on her best clothes and called on the chief of police, saying that her brother had been unjustly accused and beseeching his release.

The chief of police found her exceedingly beautiful and said he would release her brother if she would allow him to have his will of her.

'If it must be so,' she replied, 'thou must come to my house and sit and rest the whole day there.'

'And where is thy house?' he asked.

'In such-and-such a place,' she answered, and set a time for their meeting.

Then she left him and went to the Cadi of the city.

'Oh my lord the Cadi, I have a beloved brother on whose account I have come to thee. On the evidence of a false witness, the chief of police hath imprisoned him. I beseech it of thee to intercede for him with the chief of police.'

'Come to my house,' said the Cadi, 'that I may have my desire of thee, for thou pleasest me, and I will pay his forfeit myself.'

'If it must be,' said she, 'it would be better and safer for me and for thee in my house.'

'And where is thy house?'

She told him the place and appointed the same time as for the chief of police.

Then she went to the Vizier, with whom the same conversation occurred, and the same arrangement was made with him as with the two others.

Then she went to the King, who fell in love with her on the spot. He too wished her to come to him, but she asked for the honour of his so illustrious company at her house.

165

'We will not cross thee in this,' said the King. The appointment was made as for the previous ones.

Then she left him and went to a carpenter. 'I would have thee make me a cabinet,' she said, 'with four compartments, each with its door to lock up. Let me know thy hire, and I will give it to thee.'

'My hire will be four dinars,' he replied, 'but, Oh noble lady, if thou wilt vouchsafe me thy favours, I will ask nothing else of thee.'

'If thou wilt have it so,' she said, 'then make the cabinet with five compartments, each to lock up.'

'It is well. Sit down, Oh my lady, and I will make it for thee straight away, and I will come to thee at my leisure.'

She gave him the time and the place as with the others, and when the cabinet was finished had it carried to her home.

When it was the appointed time, she donned her costliest apparel and spread the room with rich rugs and then sat down to await who should come.

The Cadi was the first. She jested and toyed with him, but by and by he would have his desire, and she said, 'Oh my lord, take off thy clothes and turban and put on this yellow cassock, while I bring thee meat and drink, and after that thou shalt do as thou wishest.'

So he did, but hardly had he changed his dress when there was a knocking at the door.

'Who is that?' he asked.

'My husband!'

'What is to be done, where shall I go!'

'Fear nothing,' she said. 'I will hide thee in this cabinet.'

She took him by the hand and led him to the lowest compartment. Then she locked the door on him.

Then she went to the door and found the chief of police. She led him in and made him sit down.

'Oh my lord,' she said, 'I am thy handmaid and thou shalt pass all this day with me and sleep with me. Take off thy clothes and put on this red gown, for it is a sleeping gown.'

166

He did so, and they sported a while, but then she said to him, 'Oh lord, first of thy favour and grace write me an order for my brother's release, so that my heart may be at ease.'

'I hear and obey,' he answered, and he wrote a letter to his treasurer instructing him to set the man free without any delay whatsoever.

She took it from him and put it away. Then she returned to him, but behold! someone knocked at the door.

'Who is that?'

'My husband!'

'What shall I do?'

'Enter this cabinet till I send him away.'

So she clapped him into the second compartment and locked the door on him. And all this time the Cadi heard what they said and did.

Then she went to the door, whereupon the Vizier entered. He was given a blue cassock. Presently there came a knocking at the door.

She put him in the third compartment and locked the door on him.

After this, she opened the door and in came the King.

The usual thing happened. The King was given a patched gown, and when the knocking of the presumed husband was heard, he was led to the fourth compartment and locked in.

The lady opened the door and the carpenter entered.

'What sort of cabinet is this?' she demanded of him.

'What is wrong with it, Oh my lady?'

'The top compartment is too narrow.'

'Not so,' he said.

'Go in thyself and see. It is not wide enough.'

'It is wide enough for four people!' he said, and entered the fifth compartment. Whereupon she locked the door on him.

Then she took the letter from the chief of police and carried it to the treasurer, who delivered her lover to her. She told him all that had passed.

He said, 'And how shall we do now?'

'We will remove hence to another city, for there is no tarrying for us here after this.'

So they packed their goods and loaded them on camels, and set out immediately.

Meanwhile the five abode in the cabinet. At last the carpenter could retain his water no longer. He made water on the King's head, and the King made water on the Vizier's head, and the Vizier on the chief of police, who did the same to the Cadi. The latter cried out, 'What filth is this?'

The chief of police recognised his voice and greeted him; the Vizier the voice of the chief of police; the King recognised that of the Vizier. And they fell to talking to each other and cursing the woman.

Presently the neighbours, seeing the house deserted, broke in and discovered the starving and moaning men in the cabinet. They fetched a carpenter who opened the five doors and let the men out. Each fell to laughing when he saw how the others were attired. They sent to their people for fresh clothes and stole away, hiding from the sight of the folk.

ABDUL THE BULBUL EMIR

In the harems of Egypt no infidels see
The women more fairer than fair,
But the fairest, a Greek, was owned by a sheik
Called Abdul the Bulbul Emir.

A travelling brothel came into town,
Run by a pimp from afar
Whose great reputation had travelled the nation,
'Twas Ivan Skavinsky Skavar.

Abdul the Bulbul arrived with his bride,
A prize whose eyes shone like a star.
He claimed he could score a hundred times more
Than Ivan Skavinsky Skavar.

A great f***king contest was set for the day
A visit was planned by the Czar,
And the kerbs were all lined with harlots inclined
In honour of Ivan Skavar.

They met on the track with their ammunition slack,
Dressed only in shoes and a leer.
Both were fast on the rise, but they gasped at the size
Of Abdul the Bulbul Emir.

They worked through the night till the dawn's early light.
The clamour was heard from afar.
The multitudes came to applaud the ball game
Of Abdul and Ivan Skavar.

When Ivan had finished he turned to the Greek
And laughed when she shook with great fear.
He was puffed up with pride, and he buggered the bride
Of Abdul the Bulbul Emir.

When Ivan was done and was wiping his gun,
He bent down to polish his gear.
He felt at his back a sudden attack,
'Twas Abdul the Bulbul Emir.

Then the crowds looking on proclaimed he had won.
They were ordered to part by the Czar.
But fast were they jammed. Abdul was crammed
Into Ivan Skavinsky Skavar.

Now the cream of the joke when apart they were broke
Was laughed at for years by the Czar
For Abdul the sheik left most of his beak
In Ivan Skavinsky Skavar.

The fair Grecian maiden a sad vigil keeps
With a husband whose tastes have turned queer.
She longs for the dong that used to belong
To Abdul the Bulbul Emir.

Eden, the Pearly Gates, and the Other Place

OPEN GATES

Fellows from different parts of the country were talking in a pub about the good old good times, each claiming that his home area had the biggest reputation with the weaker sex. Scotsman, Welshman all had their say, when a London man spoke up about a neighbour of his.

It seems that this chap died and went to heaven. When he knocked at the Pearly Gates, Saint Peter looked out and asked, 'Who art thou?'

'Hoo-Ray Hercules.'

'Just a minute,' said Saint Peter.

With that, the Saint turned away from the locked gates and walked out of sight. It was a good hour later before he reappeared.

'What's the matter?' asked Hoo-Ray, 'making me wait so long? Were you looking up my record?'

'No, my son,' said Saint Peter. 'I know thy record. I was locking up the women.'

The others around the table acknowledged defeat.

EDEN

Adam and Eve were walking in the Garden.

'Do you love me?' asked Eve.

Replied Adam nonchalantly, 'Who else?'

HEAVEN?

After a long and dedicated life of teaching, a pious and venerable wise man died a peaceful death.

Years later, his most devoted follower also departed this life. On arriving at the other side, he went searching for his old teacher, and was delighted to find him sitting on a soft cloud with a beautiful blonde on his lap.

'Oh my master!' he exclaimed. 'How wonderful! I am more happy than I can express to see that you've been given your just reward!'

'Reward, my foot!' growled the old man. 'I'm her punishment.'

THE OTHER PLACE

Because a big revival meeting was being held, one winter all the lodging-houses were filled with preachers.

The small son of the owner of one of the lodging-houses came in from the cold and found the parlour crowded with preachers. He announced to them that he had dreamed of hell.

One of them grinned at him and asked what it was like.

'Just about like here,' said the boy. 'I almost froze.'

'You froze?'

'Yep, the preachers were so thick around the fire, no one else could get near it.'

AT THE PEARLY GATES

Saint Peter to new arrival: My son, what did you die of?
   Man: The Big H.
   Saint Peter: Oh, the heart! Alas, so many people are dying of heart ailments. Come in, my son.
   Next day he asks another new arrival what he died of.
   Man: The Big L.
   Saint Peter: The liver, ah yes. Come in, my son.
   Next day he asks the same question of a girl arrival.
   Girl: The Big G.
   Saint Peter: But, my daughter, you don't die of gonorrhoea!
   Girl: Oh yes you do, if you give it to my boyfriend Leroy.

THE GATES AGAIN

There is a knocking at the Pearly Gates, and God calls out, 'Who's there?'
   'It is I, Oh Lord.'
   'Oh, another goddamn English teacher.'

IT WAS HELL, ALL RIGHT

This man went through the Gates and couldn't believe his eyes. The fellows were sitting at tables with big mugs of beer in front of them, and the prettiest girls you ever saw were keeping them company.

He went and sat down next to a girl and he began right away to sweet talk her. 'Let's you and me take our beer,' he said, 'and go off where we can be alone.'

A man at the next table said, 'Hi, stranger.'

Our man said to him, 'Hi yourself. This Heaven sure is a great place. Beautiful girls and plenty to drink!'

'Take it easy, friend,' said the other fellow. 'You haven't noticed it yet, but all the beer-mugs here have holes in their bottoms, and all the girls haven't.'

THE DEVIL'S DUE

They say that when the arch-diplomat Macchiavelli was dying in Florence, a Cardinal stayed at his bedside, repeatedly urging him to renounce the devil.

But Macchiavelli whispered, 'Now is not the time to make enemies.'

HEDGING THE BET

An old woman put it in different words. She bowed her head politely every time the hell-fire preacher in church mentioned the devil, until some of the church folks asked her how come.

'I always believe in getting along with both sides,' she said, 'because you can't never tell which way the chips is going to fall.'

A TEXAN AT THE GATES

J.R. arrived at the Pearly Gates and was setting forth the reasons why he should get into heaven. Saint Peter talked with him for a while, but all J.R. was doing was to jingle his spurs and brag up Texas.

Finally Saint Peter opened the Gates and said, 'Well, you can come in. But after what you've been telling me, I'm afraid you won't like it here.'

ANOTHER TEXAN

So when another Texan came along, they were ready for him.

They asked him where he came from. 'I was born and raised in Texas,' he said.

The angel opened up the Gates. 'Come right in, brother,' he said. 'You've been in Hell long enough.'

(Everyone laughs at this story except Texans. They say they don't see anything funny in it.)

THIRD TEXAN

(Texans don't think this one is funny, either.)

This time another Texan came along, and when he got up to the big Gates, they were wide open, so he could see what was going on inside.

The Texan stood there fanning himself with his big hat, and he said, 'Gosh, I didn't know Heaven was so much like Texas.'

The gatekeeper just looked at him kind of sorrowfully. 'Son,' he said, 'this isn't Heaven.'

The fellows from Texas can fiddle and fight, knock up and throw down. They can holler loud, shoot straight, and jump high. But it seems most of them are kind of dumb when it comes to appreciating a story.

ENOUGH SAID

Why did God make Adam first?
Because he didn't want any suggestions.

THE CREATION OF EVE

When God made Eve, he left her without holes, so he gave the Devil permission to finish her. The Devil called on four assistants: a butcher, a harness-maker, a mason and a cooper.

The butcher was so clumsy, she bled. The harness-maker was no better, he put the stuffing on the outside. The mason put the cabinets of ease too near the reception room. But the cooper corrected the butcher's error, so the flood-gates now let all kinds of streams out – and in.

The Devil summed it all up. He said, 'God was a bad engineer. He put the ignition too near the exhaust.'

EVE AGAIN

Eve complained to God that she had to look after her child for a very long time, while on the other hand a mother goat is quickly free of her kid.

God said, 'You can do the same, but the goat goes to the buck only once a year.'

Eve stopped complaining.

ADAM AND EVE

Once when Adam and Eve and their children were out walking, they passed the locked gates of the Garden of Eden. The children looked in through the palings and exclaimed with delight over the singing birds and all those fruit trees and pretty flowers.

Adam told them, 'Me and your mother used to live in that place before you were born.'

One of the children asked, 'How come we aren't there now?'

Adam laughed. 'Well, the fact of the matter is, your mammy ate us out of house and home.'

LESSONS FOR ADAM

It was the final day of Creation. God woke Adam up and told him he had made a woman out of Adam's rib.

'What's a woman, God?'

God explains. 'Now, Adam,' he says, 'go and cuddle her.'

'What's a cuddle, God?'

God explains.

Next morning Adam comes back, very pleased. 'That was smashing!'

'Fine,' says God. 'Now go and practise kissing Eve.'

'What's kissing?'

God explains.

Next morning Adam is back, very very pleased. 'Kissing's smashing.'

God says, 'Well, Adam, you can now go and multiply. You needn't call again.'

'What's multiplying, God?'

God explains, and Adam goes off, very happy.

Next morning Adam appears again.

'I thought I told you not to come back, Adam.'

'But what's a headache, God?'

ETHNIC JOKE

An Irishman, a Jew and a Greek were outside the Pearly Gates, begging Saint Peter to let them in. 'No,' he said, again and again.

'Why?'

'Because,' said the Saint, turning first to the Irishman, 'you're too fond of drink. And you,' now turning to the Jew, 'you're too fond of money. And you,' turning to the Greek, 'you're too fond of sex.'

They all swore that for one more chance on earth they would do anything. They'd never sin again. The Irishman would take no drink, the Jew would take no money, and the Greek no sex – ever! Each of them solemnly promised.

At last Saint Peter said, 'Well, all right. Off you go, but if any one of you backslides, then zzztt! Like that, he'll find himself in the other place.'

The next thing they knew, they were falling through the air, and soon they landed back on earth, in a city, right in front of a pub.

'Come on!' cried the Irishman, 'Let's go in. Here's our chance to celebrate!'

The other two warned him, but he wouldn't listen, so they all went in and ordered drinks. The Irishman just started on his, and zzztt!

He vanished. He completely disappeared.

The money for the drinks fell to the floor. Then the Jew stooped down to pick it up, and zzztt!

The Greek vanished.

P.S. TO ETHNIC JOKE

What's a queer in Ireland?
  A man who prefers women to drink.

CREATION

God made man and gave him twenty years of normal sex life. At the same time he made the monkey and gave him twenty years of sex life too. But the monkey said he didn't want twenty, he just wanted ten, so God gave the extra ten to man.

  The same thing happened with the lion. He said he didn't want twenty, so God gave his extra ten to man. And the same thing happened with the donkey; man got his extra ten too.

  This explains why man has twenty years of normal sex, ten years of monkeying around, ten years of lying about it, and ten years of making an ass of himself.

HANS CARVEL

Hans Carvel, poor fellow, was worried about his wife. She was double-crossing him with other men, and he didn't know what he could do about it. He lost his appetite, couldn't work, and was unable to sleep.

Lying beside his wife one night, he managed at last to fall off into a fitful slumber in which he had a marvellous dream.

The Devil came to him and said, 'Hans, my friend, I know your trouble, and I will help you.'

'How can you help me?' asked Hans.

'Here,' said the Devil, 'I give you this ring. You must slip it on your finger. There you are! It fits. Now as long as you wear it, your wife will be faithful to you alone.'

Hans thanked him with tears of joy, and then fell into deep sleep.

In the morning he was awakened by his angry wife – and remembered his dream –

What was the ring the dawn would bring?
He blushed, for his hand was pressed
In passion's nest . . .
And then Hans sorrowfully knew
His dream was true.

OTHER PLACE

He: What possessed you to ask Mrs Jones how her husband was standing the heat?
 She: Why not?
 He: He died last year.

SO FAR, NO FURTHER

Enoch made it after all to the Pearly Gates. He knocked for admission.
 From inside came a voice. 'Who dat dere?'
 'Forget it!'

UNISEX

Catherine de Medici as Dauphine of France took her two children to visit the sick old king, her father-in-law, and to show them Titian's painting of Adam and Eve which hung in the king's room.
 'Which is Adam?' the little boy asked his sister.
 'You little silly!' she replied. 'You can't tell unless they're dressed.'

THE WHANG SONG

When the Lord made Father Adam,
They say he laughed and sang,
And sewed him up the belly
With a little piece of whang.

But when the Lord was finished,
He found he'd measured wrong.
For when the whang was knotted,
It was several inches long.

Said He, 'It's but eight inches,
So I think I'll let it hang.'
So he left on Adam's belly
That little piece of whang.

But when the Lord made Mother Eve,
Imagine he did snort,
When he saw that in her case,
The whang was inches short.

'It'll leave an awful gap,' said He,
But I don't give a hang.
She can fight it out with Adam
For that little piece of whang.'

So ever since that distant day
When human life began,
There's been a constant struggle
Twixt the woman and the man.

Women swear they'll have the pieces
That from our bellies hang,
To fill the shortages left when
The Lord ran out of whang.

But if you asked the women
And the men, they would agree
They'd rather go on struggling
Through all eternity.

THE FARMER'S CURST WIFE

There was an old man at the foot of the hill,
If he hasn't moved away, he's living there still.
Sing hi, diddle-eye, diddle-eye, fie!
Hi diddle-eye, diddle-eye day!

He hitched up his horse and he went out to plough,
But how to get around he didn't know how.
Sing hi, etc.

The Devil came to his house one day,
Said, 'One of your family I'm going to take away.'
Sing hi, etc!

'It's neither you nor your oldest son,
But your scolding wife, she is the one.'
Sing hi, etc.

'Take her on, take her on, with the joy of my heart.
I hope by golly you'll never part!'
Sing hi, etc.

The Devil put her in a sack,
And the old man says, 'Don't you bring her back.'
Sing hi, etc.

He hadn't got more than half his road,
Said 'Old woman, you are a hell of a load.'
Sing hi, etc.

He set her down for to have a little rest,
And she up with a stick and hit him her best.
Sing hi, etc.

When the Devil got her to the gates of Hell,
He said, 'Build up the fire, want to scorch her well.'
Sing hi, etc.

In come a little devil a-dragging a chain,
She upped with a hatchet and split out his brain.
Sing hi, etc.

Another little devil went climbing the wall,
Crying, 'Take her back, Daddy, she's a murdering us all!'
Sing hi, etc.

The old man was a-peeping out the crack,
And saw the old Devil come a-wagging her back.
Sing hi, etc.

She found the old man sick in bed,
She upped with the butterstick and paddled his head.
Sing hi, etc.

The old woman went whistling over the hill.
'The Devil wouldn't have me, so I wonder who will?'
Sing hi, etc.

Now you see what a woman can do,
She can best the Devil and her husband too.
Sing hi, etc.

There's one advantage women have over men:
They can go to Hell and come back again.
Sing hi, etc.

Minder

A NOVEL BY ANTHONY MASTERS

Based on the popular television series

TERRY AND ARTHUR ARE BACK!

ARTHUR:
'My word is my bond. And I'll let Terry fight to the death to prove it.'

TERRY:
'Not that I'd call Arthur mean, but when you have a drink with him he just buys the crisps!'

Arthur's the one with the silver tongue, he could talk his way past St. Peter if he wanted to. Terry's the rented muscle, the one Arthur uses to do the tidying up. Trouble is, for Terry and Arthur there's usually a sting in the tail . . .

TV TIE-IN   0 7221 5824 6   £1.50

LEONARD ROSSITER

THE LOWEST FORM OF WIT

Sarcasm is the lowest form of wit – no one is beneath using it – but it is also the most satisfying. There is no greater pleasure than pinning your squirming victim to the dinner-table with a carefully sharpened and coolly aimed insult or flooring him with a sudden and crippling kick beneath the belt.

Sarcasm requires deadly accuracy and perfect timing. It is the most skilful kind of unarmed combat and because no holds are barred it is also the most dangerous. THE LOWEST FORM OF WIT is a complete handbook for aspiring masters and mistresses of sarcasm compiled by Leonard Rossiter, a black belt of this vicious art. He tells you everything you need to know about sarcasm from its low-down role in history to specific advice on dealing with traffic wardens, bank managers, neighbours, foreigners and other despicable persons.

This is a treasury of biting jibes and stinging retorts which explores the lowest kind of wit in the highest kind of style.

HUMOUR   0 7221 7513 2   £1.50

HARRY'S OUT – AND HE'S OUT FOR REVENGE . . .

Brotherly Love

WILLIAM BLANKENSHIP

Ben and Harry are identical twins, but there the likeness ends. The brothers' bond is only skin deep: at heart one is a straightforward man . . . and one is a crazed psychopathic killer.

While Ben married, had children, became an ordinary family man, Harry did nineteen years for rape and murder. Now Harry's out to make Ben pay for those nineteen lost years. He's out to hit Ben where it hurts most – through his wife and children.

Police records show that Harry is dead. But Ben knows his psychopathic double is alive, waiting in the shadows, out for revenge, twisted and crazy enough to kill . . .

BROTHERLY LOVE

– a shattering journey into the dark side of the mind.

ADVENTURE/THRILLER   0 7221 1654 3   £1.95

BLOOD
DEEP
Colin Stubbington

A wrecked U-boat drifts into the stormy shallows off
Britain's North Sea coast. U-31's reeking hull gives up a
grisly cargo – and a clue to the Kaiser's most secret plan
– to draw Greece into the raging conflict consuming
northern Europe . . . *against the Allies!*

In the savage wake of Jutland the British are cautious
about their battleships. They can only risk sending the
mighty Aegean Squadron into Piraeus harbour if the
seas are free of steel sharks. Ralph Caradoc's mission is
to find the hidden U-boat base and blast it to kingdom
come. But his old friend Kapitan-Leutnant Kirbschaus'
mission is to send the Aegean Squadron to the bottom
of the clear blue sea . . .

WAR FICTION   0 7221 82295   £1.75

A SELECTION OF BESTSELLERS FROM SPHERE

FICTION

THE MISTS OF AVALON	Marion Bradley	£2.95 ☐
THE INNOCENT DARK	J. S. Forrester	£1.95 ☐
TRUE DETECTIVE	Max Allan Collins	£3.50 ☐
THE ALMIGHTY	Irving Wallace	£1.95 ☐
GREEN HARVEST	Pamela Oldfield	£1.95 ☐

FILM AND TV TIE-INS

THEY CALL ME BOOBER FRAGGLE	Michaela Muntean	£1.50 ☐
RED AND THE PUMPKINS	Jocelyn Stevenson	£1.50 ☐
THE RADISH DAY JUBILEE	Sheilah B. Bruce	£1.50 ☐
MINDER	Anthony Masters	£1.50 ☐
SHROUD FOR A NIGHTINGALE	P. D. James	£1.95 ☐

NON-FICTION

DIETING MAKES YOU FAT	Geoffrey Cannon & Hetty Einzig	£1.95 ☐
EMMA & CO	Sheila Hocken	£1.50 ☐
THE PEAUDOUCE FAMILY WELCOME GUIDE	Malcolm Hamer & Jill Foster	£2.95 ☐
TWINS	Peter Watson	£1.75 ☐
THE FRUIT AND NUT BOOK	Helena Radecka	£6.95 ☐

All Sphere books are available at your local bookshop or newsagent, or can be ordered direct from the publisher. Just tick the titles you want and fill in the form below.

Name _____

Address _____

_____

Write to Sphere Books, Cash Sales Department, P.O. Box 11, Falmouth, Cornwall TR10 9EN

Please enclose a cheque or postal order to the value of the cover price plus:

UK: 45p for the first book, 20p for the second book and 14p for each additional book ordered to a maximum charge of £1.63.

OVERSEAS: 75p for the first book and 21p per copy for each additional book.

BFPO & EIRE: 45p for the first book, 20p for the second book plus 14p per copy for the next 7 books, thereafter 8p per book.

Sphere Books reserve the right to show new retail prices on covers which may differ from those previously advertised in the text or elsewhere, and to increase postal rates in accordance with the PO.